BEAKERS, BUBBLES & the BIBLE

by Tina Houser

©2008 by Warner Press Inc Anderson, IN 46018

www.warnerpress.org

Editor: Karen Rhodes
Photography: Michael Meadows
Design & Illustrations: Christian Elden

Printed in USA

Warner Press Kids™
educate • nurture • inspire
www.warnerpress.org

Table of Contents

Special Thanks:

Heather Ferren; Heidi Johnson; Stacy, Rachel and Casey Lawson;
Missy, Reagan and Carlie Ritchie

A Note from Tina

You can't imagine the fun you are going to have and the tremendous lessons your kids are going to grab hold of when you use science experiments to teach important themes of the Bible.

One definition of science is that it is a method used in search of understanding. Let me challenge you to dive right in without hesitation. You are going to have just as much fun as the kids, and you'll never believe how much you all are going to remember! Using science experiments will more than likely become your favorite way to teach and definitely your kids' favorite way to learn. Outside of the classroom or group situation, these experiments make excellent outlines for family devotions. Gather 'round the kitchen table and get everyone involved!

I love utilizing what children are learning in school to teach biblical truth! My elementary education degree, my desire to be developmentally on target with kids, and my love for the dramatic drew me to science, a way to grab the attention of children. Once a child is amazed by an experiment, then the challenge is to draw something fundamentally and biblically sound from the experience. Sometimes that comes from what the child observes happening in the experiment and sometimes it comes from the emotions the experiment evokes.

In order to create an entire laboratory environment, I became Dr. Fran Bunsenburner. A simple lab coat and some laboratory glasses, along with a unique accent, and Dr. Bunsenburner captures the imagination of children as she teaches and performs her science experiments.

Although this book is full of science experiments, I do not attempt to explain the science behind each one. We'll leave that for the school teachers. You'll find that most scientific terms have been eliminated. The purpose of the experiments is to connect what physically happens with the scripture. The experience provides a bridge to what the Bible teaches and a way to make spiritual discoveries.

In science, we describe what we experience with our five senses: seeing, feeling, tasting, hearing and smelling. We also put things in categories, compare sizes, distances, and weights, and infer something we don't actually see. Every part of each exercise is important: performing the experiment, the observations, and the discussion.

Here are a few pointers that will make these experiments more exciting to everyone.

- Always, and I mean every time, try the experiment before showing the kids. The size of a container, the amount of water, or the time that it takes can vary when using non-standardized items you find around the house. A trial run will give you confidence in front of the children and your experiment will never "fizzle."

- Whenever possible and reasonable considering the age of the children, provide materials for them to do the experiments themselves. Experiments are exciting to watch, but they are even more intriguing to do yourself!

- Use the translation indicated with the printed scripture. Certain words used only in that translation will be beneficial in relating the experiment to the scripture.

- Follow safety precautions.

Safety Rules

- Discuss all the safety rules with the children regularly.

- Keep dangerous materials out of reach of all children.

- Don't eat, touch or taste anything in the experiment unless specifically instructed to do so by the adult leader.

- Wear safety glasses.

- Read labels completely.

God has blasted me with a gargantuan passion for reaching kids for His Kingdom. And I will do just about anything to make that a reality. Sometimes it means putting on a crazy costume. Sometimes it means coaching parents through their doubts and frustrations. Sometimes it means giving up my day off to be part of a community kids' day. Sometimes it means listening to a wildly bizarre story that is real in a child's imagination. And, sometimes it means inviting children into a make-believe laboratory hosted by Dr. Fran Bunsenburner.

Step into my laboratory and let's learn the messages God wants to deliver!

(We can also blow something up in the meantime!)

A Glass of Forgiveness
Learning Forgiveness

1 John 1:9 (KJV) - If we confess our sins, he is faithful and just to forgive us our sins, and to cleanse us from all unrighteousness.

Lab Equipment

- candle
- clear drinking glass (taller than the candle)
- coin
- flat plate
- food coloring
- match
- water

Before You Begin

- Test this experiment before showing it to the children to determine the amount of water that will work well with your particular plate.

- Add food coloring to the water in order for it to show up against the plate.

Experiment

- Place the candle in the center of the plate and light it.

- Set the coin on the plate several inches from the candle. Pour enough colored water around the candle so that it completely covers the bottom of the plate where the coin is.

- Place the clear drinking glass over the candle and watch.

- When the flame goes out on the candle, the water will be drawn into the glass, leaving the coin by itself on the plate.

Observation

- What happened to the flame when the glass was placed over the candle?

- What happened to the water that was around the coin?

Discussion

- Each one of these things in our experiment represents something. The candle is God, the water is you, the coin is sin and the glass is when God forgives you. (The flame itself has no significance.)

- With these representations in mind, repeat the experiment asking questions as you go. Ask the significance of each item as you put it in place. When the candle, water, and coin are in place, ask where the sin (coin) is. It is in you (water).

- Read 1 John 1:9. The Bible tells us that if we confess our sin, God will forgive us for disobeying Him. When we confess our sin, there is something different about our lives. What is different about where the sin (coin) is once God forgives us?

- When God forgives us He pulls us away from our sin and close to Him. He doesn't want that sin to be part of our lives anymore.

Balancing Forks
Life's Balance

Psalm 119:106-112 (NLT) - I've promised it once, and I'll promise again: I will obey your wonderful laws. I have suffered much, O Lord; restore my life again, just as you promised. Lord, accept my grateful thanks and teach me your laws. My life constantly hangs in the balance, but I will not stop obeying your law.

The wicked have set their traps for me along your path, but I will not turn from your commandments. Your decrees are my treasure; they are truly my heart's delight. I am determined to keep your principles, even forever, to the very end.

Lab Equipment

• 2 identical table forks
• old magazine
• sharpened pencil
• tall beverage glass
• very small potato

Experiment

• Push the pencil all the way through the potato. Don't hold the potato in your hand, but put it against a magazine or stack of newspapers as you push on the pencil.

• Push the tines of a fork into the potato so that the fork is hanging down and out. Now, push another in the opposite side of the potato at the same angle hanging down and out. (Refer to photo.)

• Turn the glass upside down and rest the point of the pencil on the bottom, forks off to each side. Adjust the forks so that the whole thing balances completely on the point of the pencil. By changing the position of the forks, you can make the pencil lean to one side or stand up straight.

Observation

> WHAT IS EQUAL ON BOTH SIDES OF THE POTATO?

- What was the most difficult part of preparing the experiment?

- What was the entire thing able to rest on?

- What happened when you changed the position of the forks?

Discussion

- What do you think would happen if you replaced one of the forks with a much bigger fork?

- We can describe our lives as being in balance. How do we balance our lives?

- When sin tries to weigh us down on one side, what do we need to do? (The sin will get us off-balance so we need to get rid of it. When we get down or frustrated about something and it adds weight to one side, then we need to remember all the goodness of God to add to the other side. His goodness always outweighs the frustration.)

- Read Psalm 119:106-112. What does it say about balance? When do we have to think about keeping our lives in balance? (It's something we have to think about all the time.)

- How does the person writing these verses keep his life spiritually balanced? (He remembers that God's words are his treasure and delight. He promises to keep God's decrees or live by God's law. Also, he is thankful and reminds himself of God's greatness and faithfulness. Those reminders and promises keep you in balance when you're tempted by Satan.)

Balloon Zip Line
Focus

Philippians 4:8 (NLT) - *And now, dear brothers and sisters, let me say one more thing as I close this letter. Fix your thoughts on what is true and honorable and right. Think about things that are pure and lovely and admirable. Think about things that are excellent and worthy of praise.*

Lab Equipment

- 6-foot long string
- balloon
- scissors
- straw
- tape

Experiment

- Blow the balloon up, but do not tie it. Let it loose in the room and watch where it goes.

- Cut the straw so it is 4"-5" long.

- Now, blow up the balloon a second time. This time, tape a straw to one side of the balloon. Thread the string through the straw.

- One person will hold one end of the string. Another person will hold the other end of the string with the balloon close to the end. (The balloon is still inflated but not tied off.) The mouth of the balloon should be resting against the person's hand.

- Make sure the string is pulled taut and then release the balloon. It should sail along the string to the other person.

Observation

• Where did the balloon go when it was released into the room the first time?

• Where did the balloon go when it was released the second time?

• Which flight demonstrated focus?

• With which flight were you able to tell where the balloon would go?

Discussion

• Read Philippians 4:8. This verse tells us eight things that God instructs us to focus our thoughts on. Name the eight things. Go through each one and make sure the children understand the meaning of the words. If not, exercise your dictionary skills and look up the words in question.

• If we are focused on what is true, honorable, right, pure, lovely, admirable, excellent, and praiseworthy, then we know that we are headed in the direction that God wants us to go. Which balloon was most like focusing on what God wants us to think about?

• Which ones of the things listed in Philippians 4:8 does Satan like? None of them! What happens if we decide not to do the honorable thing? Which one of the balloons would that be like? What happens if we decide to tell a lie instead of the truth?

• When we focus on godly things, like in Philippians 4:8, we are moving in a direction that points us to God, just like the balloon went straight from one end of the string to the other. When we don't pay attention to godly things, then are lives get confusing and we don't know where we're going or what we are doing–just like the balloon that was let go in the room. We had no idea where it was going to land.

Being See-Through
All-Knowing

John 8:6 (NLT) - *They were trying to trap him into saying something they could use against him, but Jesus stooped down and wrote in the dust with his finger.*

Lab Equipment

- eyedroppers
- liquid watercolor paints
- plain gelatin
- small cups
- spray cooking oil
- Styrofoam™ bowl
- water
- waxed paper

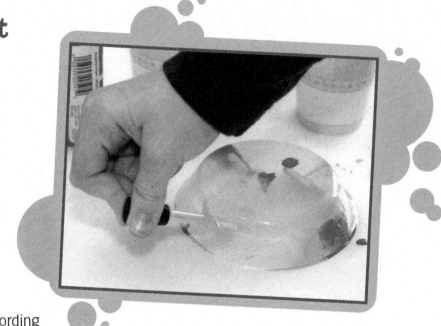

Experiment

- Dissolve the plain gelatin according to the directions on the package.

- Lightly spray the inside of the Styrofoam™ bowls with spray cooking oil and fill with the dissolved gelatin. Refrigerate overnight.

- Turn the bowl upside-down and remove the gelatin form. Place it on a piece of waxed paper.

- Pour several colors of the paint into small cups and provide an eyedropper for each color.

- Fill the eyedropper with paint by placing the tip in the paint and then squeezing the bulb. When you release the bulb, the paint will fill the tube. Now, poke the eyedropper into the gelatin at any point and squirt the paint. Add different colors of paint, but use only the eyedropper that accompanies that paint color. Try wiggling the eyedropper back and forth as you squeeze and pull it out.

- You'll be able to see the colorful design you created inside the gelatin.

Observation

- Did some of the colors bleed into one another? Which ones? What happened when they touched one another?

- Look at the design that was created. Does it remind you of anything? What? (Maybe a spider, butterfly, fingers or worms)

Discussion

- Why were you able to see the paints? (The gelatin is transparent; you can see through it.)

- Tell the children the story from John 8:1-11. Jesus was teaching in the temple, but some people called Pharisees didn't like what Jesus was saying. They were trying to trick Jesus into saying something they could arrest Him for. One day they brought a woman to Jesus who had broken one of the commandments God had given the people. The law said she should be stoned to death for what she did. The Pharisees asked Jesus what He thought they should do. Jesus knew what they were trying to do. He knew they were trying to trick Him so He just stooped down and starting writing in the sand. That really made the Pharisees angry. They wanted an answer! Finally, Jesus looked up and told them that the person who had not sinned could be the first one to throw a stone. Then He went back to writing in the sand. One-by-one the men left until everyone was gone but the woman. Jesus' question had caused them to think about how they had disobeyed God's commandments. With no one left to accuse her, Jesus told the woman to leave and not sin anymore.

- Jesus could see right through the Pharisees so He knew what they were trying to do. It was as if they were clear. The gelatin was clear so we could see what was actually going on when the paint was squirted. Jesus can also see through us. He knows when we are doing something to draw attention to ourselves because He can see into our hearts. He knows when we do something that we hope will cause someone else to get her feelings hurt. Jesus knows our motives because He knows our hearts and our minds.

- What does Jesus see when He looks at you?

Clean Up

Clean the eyedroppers out immediately with warm soapy water. Squeeze the bulb repeatedly in the water to bring soapy water in and out quickly. This will clean the paint out of the eyedropper.

Blob in the Dark
Light

Psalm 18:28 (NLT) - *Lord, you have brought light to my life; my God, you light up my darkness.*

Lab Equipment

- ¼ teaspoon Glow Powder (See "Supply Sites" to order this)
- lamp
- tablespoon
- test tube with a cap
- vegetable oil
- water

Experiment

- Measure ¼ teaspoon of the glow powder and put it inside the test tube.

- Add 1 tablespoon of water to the test tube. Gently swirl the water around in the bottom of the test tube so the glow powder and water mix.

- Fill the test tube the rest of the way with vegetable oil. You don't want any room for air, so get it as full as you can without making a mess. Screw on the cap.

- Turn the test tube sideways and hold it up against the light for at least 30 seconds. Turn out all the lights and gently move the test tube so that the blob moves around. The blob now glows in the dark!

Observation

- Describe the test tube when the lights were turned out.

- What was the blob doing when it was held up to the lamp?

- After talking about it the first week, let the test tube sit undisturbed until the next week. Then, hold it up to the lamp and then turn out the lights. Has anything changed?

Discussion

• What did the lamp give to the blob?

• Read Psalm 18:28. What brings light to our lives?

• How does God bring light to our lives? (When light comes into a room, we can see things we couldn't see before.) What can you see about yourself once you start having a relationship with God? (An investigator takes a flashlight around a room looking for anything that could help him figure out what happened. It might be a tiny little thing he notices that helps him solve the mystery. As we study God's Word, we find even small things about our lives that we need to hand over to God so that He can help us change.)

• What has God shown you? What has He lit up in your life? Have you had a wrong attitude toward someone? Have you gotten into a bad habit? Do you think more highly of yourself than you ought to? Are you honoring your parents by obeying them? Name some other things that God can reveal with His light.

Blow, Blow, Blow!
Salvation

1 John 1:9 (NLT) - *But if we confess our sins to him, he is faithful and just to forgive us and to cleanse us from every wrong.*

Lab Equipment

• empty pop bottle
• small piece of paper

Experiment

• Make a tight little paper wad with the piece of paper. It should be smaller than the opening to the pop bottle.

• Set the paper wad on a table and place your chin against the table, so you will be able to blow the paper wad. Now, get a friend to hold the empty pop bottle so that the opening to the bottle is against the table and about a foot away from where you are blowing. Blow the paper wad into the bottle. I said, blow the paper wad into the bottle. Come on, you can do it ... just blow the paper wad into the bottle!

• The bottle is full of unseen air and won't permit anything else to enter.

Observation

- Could you make the paper wad go into the pop bottle?

- Were you blowing too hard? Not hard enough?

- Why would it not go inside the bottle? Was there something else in the bottle? (There was already air in the bottle. When you blew toward the bottle, it kept the air inside, so the paper couldn't enter. Two different things [like the air and the paper] cannot take up the same space at the same time.)

Discussion

- Think about how this experiment is like God coming into our lives. Before He can come in, something has to get out. What needs to get out of our lives? (sin) God is perfect and is not present in sin, so He offers us a way to get rid of the sin, by offering us forgiveness. He can then come into our lives. Read 1 John 1:9.

- How do we get sin out of our lives? (We pray, ask God for forgiveness, and put our trust in Jesus. Don't just say you're sorry, but ask God to help you change your attitudes, your words, your thoughts and your actions.)

- Provide a time when a child can make this decision to accept God. A few things to keep in mind, though, when talking to a child about salvation: The fact that they are asking questions does not necessarily mean they are ready to make a life-changing decision. Questions are very natural for children, and that's how they proceed from knowing a little to understanding a lot. Use words the child will understand; avoid "religious" words and symbolism.

Bubble Maker
God's Greatness

2 Chronicles 2:6 (NLT) - *But who can really build him a worthy home? Not even the highest heavens can contain him! So who am I to consider building a Temple for him, except as a place to burn sacrifices to him?*

Lab Equipment

- 2 empty 20-ounce plastic bottles (from pop or water)
- a large clear drinking glass filled two-thirds full with water
- bubble solution
- small dish (custard cup or pot pie pan)

Experiment

- Beforehand, place two 20-ounce plastic bottles in the freezer. Place one of the bottles from the freezer into a clear drinking glass that has been filled two-thirds with water. The mouth of the bottle should be down. Watch what happens. (It should blow some underwater bubbles.)

- Make some bubble solution by adding 4 drops of dish soap to each ¼ cup of water used or use some store-bought bubble solution.

- Pour a little of the bubble solution into the small dish. Now, take the other bottle out of the freezer. Dip the mouth of the bottle into the bubble solution and set the bottle upright. Watch what happens. (It should blow a bubble.) Each time a bubble breaks dip the bottle in the solution again. It will continue doing this until the bottle warms up close to room temperature.

Observation

- What happened when you put the frozen bottle under water?

- What happened when you dipped the frozen bottle in the bubble solution?

Discussion

• What do the bubbles under the water and the bubbles on top of the bottle have inside them? (air)

• Where did that air come from? (inside the bottle)

• Why did it come out? (There wasn't enough room for it. The bottle couldn't hold all the air, because as it warmed up, it took up more space.)

• Read 2 Chronicles 2:6. You may also want to read the story "Solomon Builds the Temple" from *EGERMEIER'S® BIBLE STORY BOOK* to get a better feel for the context of this verse.

• What did Solomon say about God in this verse? (He is greater and there is more to God than can be held in a building. God is even greater than the highest heavens!)

• How is our experiment like this verse that we just read? What could the bottle represent? What could the air represent? (The air could not be held in the bottle and man cannot keep God contained.)

Caught Off Balance
Saul's Conversion

Acts 9:21 (*The Message*) - *They were caught off guard by this and, not at all sure they could trust him, they kept saying, "Isn't this the man who wreaked havoc in Jerusalem among the believers? And didn't he come here to do the same thing—arrest us and drag us off to jail in Jerusalem for sentencing by the high priests?"*

Lab Equipment

• a sturdy smooth board or cookie sheet
• four 9-inch balloons

Experiment

• Blow up the four balloons so they are all close in size. Don't blow them up until they are stretched to the max, but about three-quarters full of air is sufficient.

• Cluster the balloons on the floor and place the smooth board on top of them. The children may think the board itself will break the balloons, but it won't.

• Choose a child to stand on the board. This can be done either of two ways. One adult can lift the child while another adult steadies him or her with one hand, and then gently stands the child on the board so that both feet come down together. Or, the child can hold an adult's hand for balance and place one foot on the board, pulling the other foot up to the board so he or she is standing. The balloons don't break!

Observation

- What were you expecting to happen? Why did this seem impossible? (It's a lot of weight to go on balloons that are so fragile.)

- Did the balloons pop?

- Was the person at ease (and balanced) as soon as they stepped up on the board or did it take a moment to adjust?

- Try someone a little heavier and see what happens.

Discussion

- What made this experiment amazing? (We weren't expecting the balloons to support a person without popping.)

- What did it take for you to believe that the balloons would support the weight? (see the proof)

- Read Acts 9:1-31 from THE MESSAGE.

- What caught the people in Jerusalem off balance or off guard about Saul?

- What did it take for the apostles to accept Saul as a believer? (see the proof)

- The difference in Saul, from the time he ferociously persecuted Christians until after he became a believer himself, was so drastic it was difficult for the followers in Jerusalem to believe he had really changed. It caught them "off balance" because the change was so unexpected! Saul kept preaching boldly about Jesus, which finally convinced the Christians that he was telling them the truth.

Cleansing Blood
Sacrifice

Hebrews 9:13-14 (NLT) - *Under the old system, the blood of goats and bulls and the ashes of a young cow could cleanse people's bodies from ritual defilement. Just think how much more the blood of Christ will purify our hearts from deeds that lead to death so that we can worship the living God. For by the power of the eternal Spirit, Christ offered himself to God as a perfect sacrifice for our sins.*

Lab Equipment

- 2 UNCOATED laxative pills (Exlax®)
- blunt object to grind with
- custard dish
- soap
- spoon
- tablespoon of rubbing alcohol

Experiment

- Crush the 2 laxative pills in the custard dish. Pour in the rubbing alcohol and thoroughly mix.

- Rub the mixture on your hands and let this dry completely.

- When your hands are dry, wash them off with soap and water. Oh my! What's happening?

- Your hands will turn bright red!

Observation

- How long did it take for the alcohol/laxative mixture to dry on your hands? What did it feel like?

- What happened when you washed your hands with soap and water?

- What color did it turn? What did this remind you of?

Discussion

• Before Jesus was crucified on the cross and resurrected, sacrifices were made in the temple. These sacrifices were animals (like goats, sheep, birds and bulls) that were killed as an offering to God for any sins that had been committed. The animal had to be the best, a perfect one. In this way the people could pay a penalty for displeasing God. This was what God had instructed them to do to be clean again. When Jesus died, His blood was the sacrifice for everyone who would believe in Him. No more would animals need to be sacrificed because God's Son had been the highest sacrifice that could ever be made. No one could ever sacrifice more than God did when He allowed Jesus to offer Himself to be crucified. God did this to show us how desperately He loves us. His willingness went beyond anything we can ever dream. There could be no more perfect sacrifice than Jesus, God's Son.

• Read Hebrews 9:13-14.

• The blood we created in this experiment was fake but the blood that came from Jesus when He died on the cross was very real. Because of the sin and disobedience of all people who have lived, Jesus offered Himself as the last and most perfect sacrifice. Because of our sin and disobedience even today, God gave His Son.

• Why did Jesus do that? (God loved us even before we were born and He wants us to live closely with Him. When we accept Jesus' sacrifice, then even though we have gone far away from God, He will celebrate our return.)

Clear as Mud
Forgiveness

1 John 1:9 (NLT) - *But if we confess our sins to him, he is faithful and just to forgive us and to cleanse us from every wrong.*

Lab Equipment

- ¼ cup of dirt
- 2 quart-size bowls
- 2 sheets of paper towel, still connected
- concrete block
- water

Experiment

- Fill one bowl about halfway with water. Stir in the dirt until the water is muddy. Set this bowl on a concrete block (or something of similar height) laying on its side.

- Place the empty bowl next to the concrete block.

- Fold the two connected pieces of paper towel in half lengthwise. Fold again, and then a third time, so that it is a long, thick strip of paper.

- Place one end of the paper towel strip down in the muddy water on top of the concrete block. The end should go all the way down in the bowl. Put the other end in the empty bowl setting next to the concrete block.

- Let the bowls set overnight. If you are doing a demonstration and want to show the results at that time, show a similar set-up that you prepared the day before.

- The water will move through the paper towel strip to the empty bowl, leaving the mud behind.

Observation

- What does the piece of paper towel feel like? What does it look like?

- What is in the bowl on top of the concrete block?

- What is in the bowl that is next to the concrete block?

- How is the water different from when the experiment started?

Discussion

- What happens when you get a piece of dirt in your eye? (it hurts) What happens when there's a piece of dirt on a CD that you're trying to listen to? (it won't play right) If you get dirt in your gasoline tank, it damages your car.

- What happens when we have sin in our lives? (We are not what God intended us to be; we don't run right!) Sin is what displeases God. Name some sins--name some things that displease God. (Encourage the children to go further than saying lying and stealing, such as treating others with disrespect, name calling, bullying, being selfish, demanding our way.)

- The Bible tells us that everyone has sinned–yes, everyone! Read 1 John 1:9. But God also gives us a way to get rid of that sin through Jesus. What does this verse say we need to do? (confess or admit our sin) Then, what does it say that God will do? (clean us up)

- How is our experiment like this verse? What part is like us when we are full of sin? What part represents what God does? What part is like us once God has forgiven us?

Corrugated Strength
God's Strength in Us

James 4:6 (NLT) - *He gives us more and more strength to stand against such evil desires.*

Lab Equipment

- 3 pieces of copy paper
- one glass jar, coffee can, or similar item

Experiment

- Wrap one piece of copy paper around the jar and tape the ends together. Pull the paper cylinder off the jar. Do this a second time with another piece of copy paper. You now have two paper cylinders.

- Set the two cylinders 4"- 5" from one another.

- Place the third piece of copy paper on top of the cylinders.

- Start to set the jar on the paper between the cylinders. Ask the children what they think will happen? (It will fall and break.)

- Now, take the piece of copy paper that was resting on top of the cylinders and fold it back and forth to corrugate it. Make the folds ¼" - ½" in width.

- Put the corrugated piece of paper back on top of the two paper cylinders so that the pleats are going from one cylinder to the other.

- Set the jar on the corrugated paper between the cylinders.

Observation

- What happened to the jar when it was set on the plain paper?

- What happened to the jar when it was set on the corrugated paper?

Discussion

- Something was added to the paper when it was folded back and forth. What was added to the paper? (strength)

- What is it called when paper is folded to add strength? (corrugate)

- Read James 4:6. Tell what this verse means in your own words.

- What represents our "evil desires" in this experiment? (the jar)

- What represents our strength? (the plain paper)

- What represents God's strength? (making the paper corrugated)

- The paper did not have strength to stand against the jar (our evil desires) when it was flat. We can't stand against all the things that Satan throws at us by ourselves. When we added the folds to the paper, it got a lot stronger. The more folds (God's strength) we added, the stronger the paper got, and it was able to hold the jar without caving in. James 4:6 tells us that as we grow closer to Him, God will give us more and more strength to face everything that Satan tries to get us to think and do.

Disappearing Sin
Forgiveness

1 John 1:7 (NLT) - *But if we are living in the light of God's presence, just as Christ is, then we have fellowship with each other, and the blood of Jesus, his Son, cleanses us from every sin.*

Lab Equipment

- piece of yellow cellophane
- piece of white paper
- yellow highlighter

Experiment

- Ask the children to tell you things that make God unhappy, things that displease Him. These are called sins. Using the yellow highlighter, write one word on the white paper that summarizes each of their contributions.

- Cover the white paper with the piece of yellow cellophane. What happened to the words that were just written?

- The yellow cellophane covered the words so they disappeared.

Observation

- What happened to the words that were written on the paper?

Discussion

• What covered up the sins that you had listed on the paper? (the yellow cellophane)

• Read 1 John 1:7.

• What does this verse say takes away our sins or cleanses us from sin? (the blood of Jesus)

• What does the yellow cellophane remind you of, then? (the blood of Jesus) Why?

• The words on the paper were sins, and when the yellow cellophane was placed over them, they disappeared. We don't place a piece of yellow cellophane over our bodies to make our sins go away. What is it that we have to do in order for our personal sin to be taken away? (We admit our sins to God. We believe that Jesus was sent by His Heavenly Father to shed His blood and take our punishment for sin. We ask God to forgive us.)

• God wants us to turn ourselves over to Him for a brand new start. He has a new life waiting for each person!

An Additional Idea

Use this same concept to help children with the story of Jesus healing the leper. Draw the outline of a man with a black marker. In front of the children put yellow dots with a yellow highlighter pen on the man for the leprosy. Lay a piece of yellow cellophane over the man when it says that Jesus healed him. The spots will disappear.

Mark 1:41-42 (NLT) - Moved with pity, Jesus touched him. "I want to," he said. "Be healed!" Instantly the leprosy disappeared—the man was healed.

Drawn to God
Unfailing Love

Psalm 119:76 – *Let, I pray thee, thy merciful kindness be for my comfort according to thy word unto thy servant.*

Hebrews 10:22 – *Let us draw near with a true heart in full assurance of faith, having our hearts sprinkled from an evil conscience, and our bodies washed with pure water.*

Lab Equipment

- bar magnet
- glass
- paper clip
- tape
- thread

SEE "SUPPLY SITES" TO ORDER THE BAR MAGNET!

Experiment

- Cut a piece of thread about a foot long and tie one end to a paper clip. Rest the bar magnet across the top of a glass so that the magnet end is sticking over the side. Place the paper clip against the under side of the magnet. It will stick there.

- Slowly begin to pull down on the thread so that the paper clip eases away from the magnet. Once there is one inch of space between the paper clip and magnet, place a piece of tape across the thread onto the table. This will hold the paper clip in place.

- The paper clip will stay suspended in mid-air as long as the magnet is not moved.

Observation

- Describe what you see.

- How long do you think the paper clip will stay like this?

- Move the magnet slightly and see what happens.

Discussion

- What is causing the paper clip to stay in mid-air?

- Will the magnet ever get tired of pulling on the paper clip?

- Read Psalm 119:76. Relate the scripture to what you see happening with the magnet and paper clip.

- God's love is unfailing; that means it never stops–no matter what we do, He will never stop loving us. He never stops wanting us to get closer to Him.

- Read Hebrews 10:22. Are we like the paper clip or the magnet? Which represents God– the paper clip or the magnet? What does this verse say we should do? (God wants us to draw close to Him.)

- What can we do to get closer to God? When do you feel drawn closest to God? Is it when you are alone in your bedroom? In worship service? With your friends? On vacation? When you're spending time with your family? God's love for you never stops, and our desire to be closer to Him should never stop.

Encourage the Flame
Encouragement

1 Peter 5:12b (NLT) - My purpose in writing is to encourage you and assure you that the grace of God is with you no matter what happens.

Lab Equipment

- 2 matches
- candle

Experiment

- Light the candle. Extinguish the match.

- Wait for about 30 seconds to let the candle burn, then light another match.

- Blow out the candle. As the stream of smoke moves upward, move the match through the smoke, gradually getting closer to the candle. The candle will reignite without the match coming close to the wick of the candle.

Observation

- What did the first match have to touch to ignite?

- What did the second match have to touch to light the candle?

- How close was the second match to the wick of the candle when it relit?

Discussion

- Let's talk about a pretend situation. There was a woman who found out that she was very sick. She had been a Christian for about two years and her faith was getting stronger every day. Until the news of her sickness, her life seemed so good; she had a wonderful family and a great job. But, when she got sick she had lots of questions and she blamed God for the difficult things in her life. If you were this woman's friend, what would you say or do to encourage her to keep relying on God?

- Do the experiment again. The candle represents people going through difficult times and the flame stands for their relationship with God. This time, tell the children to be ready to say words of encouragement when you give them the signal. Don't wait for turns, but say the encouraging words on top of one another. When you blow out the candle, signal the children, and then begin moving the match through the smoke. What helped the people's relationship with God to be relit? (your encouragement)

- When we encourage others through hard times our words and actions give them hope. God wants Christians to encourage one another and remind each other that He will be with them through the difficult times. Name some difficult things that people go through. After each thing the children name, ask how they can encourage that person. Then, remind them that God will go with you when (fill in the blank with their comment).

- Read 1 Peter 5:12b. How would you describe these words?

Evidence of Love
Actions

John 13:35 (NLT) - *Your love for one another will prove to the world that you are my disciples.*

Lab Equipment

- mini-marshmallows
- toothpicks

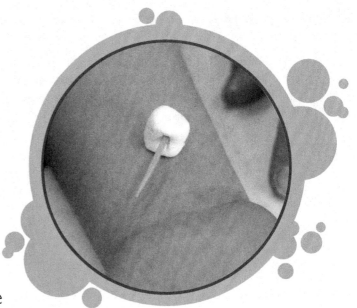

Experiment

- Write the name of each child on a craft stick and place them in a potato chip can. Draw out two sticks at a time to determine partners.

- Give each pair a mini-marshmallow and a toothpick. Break the toothpick in half and stick it into the marshmallow, but not all the way through. One child will place his arm, from the wrist to the elbow, flat against the table with palm up. His partner will feel around the wrist until she can feel the pulse. At the point where she felt the pulse she should place the marshmallow, so the toothpick is sticking out and not leaning against the child's arm. Stay very, very still and watch the toothpick closely.

- The toothpick will move ever so slightly to match the child's pulse.

- If it is difficult to see, the child can try running in place for a minute to get his heart beating a little faster to make the pulse stronger.

Observation

- How difficult was it to figure out where to set the marshmallow on the wrist?

- What do you see the toothpick doing?

- Which shows more action, the marshmallow or the toothpick?

Discussion

• What part of the body do we think of when we talk about love? (the heart)

• What does your heart actually do for your body? (pumps blood)

• How can you tell how fast your heart is pumping? (test your pulse rate)

• Why did the toothpick move? (The toothpick connected to the marshmallow moves slightly every time your heart beats. If your heart is doing what it is supposed to do and you've got the marshmallow in the right spot, the toothpick will move each time the hearts beats.)

• Read John 13:35. You know your heart is beating because you can see the evidence in the toothpick moving. Now, let's think about our spiritual heart. It is supposed to pump love through us instead of blood.

  • How do people know that we love God?

  • What evidence do they see of our love for God?

  • What evidence do they see that we love them?

  • What should we do to convince others that we love God? (When we let God use our actions to love others, then they believe in a God who could also love them. God's love is pumping through us and proving to others that He is alive and working in us.)

  • Is your pulse strong?

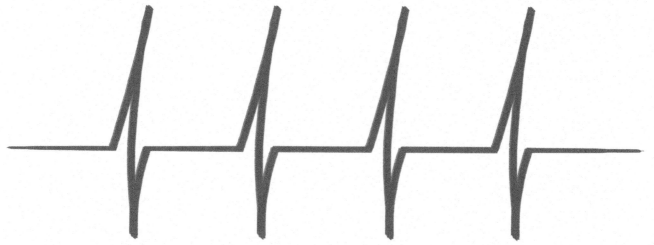

Fist Full of Rain
Miracles

1 Kings 18:41-46

Lab Equipment

- burner
- double boiler
  (or 2 pots that can rest
  on one another)
- ice
- water

Experiment

- Fill the smaller pot about halfway with cold water and add ice.

- Fill the larger pot halfway with water and bring it to a boil.

- When the water begins to boil, hold the smaller cold pot over it so the pot is directly hit by the steam. You want to be able to see the bottom of the smaller pot. Hold steady and watch what happens to the bottom of the smaller pot. (Caution: Do not put your hand close to the steam.)

- Beads of water will form and eventually there will be some raindrops.

Observation

- What change do you notice at first?

- As you keep the smaller pot over the boiling pot, what happens? (It's raining!)

- How long does it continue to do this?

Discussion

God used Elijah to prove to King Ahab that He was the One True God and that the idols they had been worshiping were worthless. But, three years earlier Elijah had prophesied that there would be a great famine.

Just as he said, the people had not seen or felt rain in over three years. Because there was no rain, the crops would not grow and the livestock starved. The people were hungry and thirsty.

Elijah climbed a mountain to pray for God to send rain. After praying for awhile, Elijah sent his servant to look toward the sea for clouds. The servant returned with word that there were no clouds. Elijah prayed again and sent his servant to look toward the sea for clouds. Again, the servant returned with bad news. Elijah did this seven times. When the servant returned the seventh time, he said that there was only one small cloud, about the size of his fist.

Elijah knew God was answering prayer and would send the rain. He came down the mountain to tell the king to return home before he got soaked! Soon the skies got dark and it rained... and rained...and rained. The ground was muddy and the rivers were full. Everyone was thankful that God had sent the rain.

- How did the servant react to seeing the little cloud? How did Elijah react when the servant told him about the little cloud? What did the little cloud mean to Elijah?

- In our experiment, we first saw the moisture gathering on the bottom of the top pot, and then it started to drip off of it. The little cloud would have made just a sprinkling of rain, but God used it to signal the coming of a downpour. Elijah got excited about the little cloud because he knew God was working and it was the first part of a miracle.

- How do you feel when you see God working in little ways? (Sometimes, He just keeps using that same situation to show us a bigger miracle.)

- Tell about a time when you knew God was working, and He blessed more than you expected.

Flash! It's Gone!
He Is Not Here!

Luke 24:5-6 (NIV) - *In their fright the women bowed down with their faces to the ground, but the men said to them, "Why do you look for the living among the dead? He is not here; he has risen! Remember how he told you, while he was still with you in Galilee.*

Lab Equipment

• clear glass pie plate
• flash paper (see "Supply Sites" to order this)
• match

Experiment

• Information about where to purchase flash paper is in the appendix. When you get it, open the package immediately. Set the paper out to dry overnight. Because it is highly flammable, it is usually shipped damp, but it needs to be completely dry to work with. Also, if not dried out immediately, it may mold.

• You will need to perform this experiment in a dark room to add to its effectiveness.

• Lay a piece of the flash paper in the center of the clear glass plate. Turn the lights out. Then, touch the edge of the flash paper with the lit match.

• Count how long it takes for the flash paper to burn.

• It burns quickly and leaves no residue!

Observation

• How long did it take for the flash paper to burn up?

• What was left in the pan when the flame went out?

• Can you locate the ashes?

Discussion

- When you light a piece of paper, it usually goes up in flames. What was different about the flash paper? Did it burn out quicker than you thought it would?

- When you burn a normal piece of paper, what is left? What was different about this paper?

- Let's think about what the Bible tells us about Jesus' death and resurrection. Jesus was killed when He was hung on a cross. He was taken down and placed in the grave belonging to Joseph of Arimethea. A stone was rolled across the opening to the grave and then later some women came to the garden where the grave was. Let's read Luke 24:5-6. What did the women find there? What did they expect to find? Were there ashes or any part of Jesus' body left in the grave? What had happened to Jesus?

- How can you relate our experiment to these verses? The paper was completely gone and Jesus' body was completely gone. It didn't take long for the paper to disappear, and Jesus didn't stay in the grave long.

Foaming Fountain
Love

1 Thessalonians 3:12 (NLT) - *And may the Lord make your love grow and overflow to each other and to everyone else, just as our love overflows toward you.*

Lab Equipment

- 2-liter of diet soft drink
- Geyser Tube (optional)
- Mentos®

Experiment

- Open the 2-liter bottle of pop. Diet works best because it's easier to clean up if you get some on you (or somewhere it shouldn't be...oops!)

- Securely fasten the Geyser Tube to the 2-liter bottle, if you are going to use it. The experiment can be done without the Geyser Tube, but its use will make the fountain go higher.

- Put the pin in place on the Geyser Tube and then load it full with Mentos®. If not using the tube, then fill your hands with Mentos® and cup them around the opening to the 2-liter bottle.

- Hold onto the bottle with one hand, and pull the pin with the other. Step back quickly and watch the white fountain of foaming pop spew into the air. If you're doing this experiment without the tube, drop the Mentos® in as quickly as possible and step back. Don't lean over the opening of the bottle, or...well... just don't.

Observation

• How much time passed after the Mentos® were released into the pop before something happened?

• How high did the foam fountain go?

• Did anyone get wet?

• How did the observers react?

• How many people wanted to see it again?

Discussion

• What do you think would have made the fountain go higher?

• Which was more interesting and exciting–the bottle of pop or the bottle of pop with Mentos® dropped in it? How did you feel when you saw the foam fountain? Was anyone sad when they saw the fountain?

• The Bible tells us that we should love one another. Describe what that love should be like. Read 1 Thessalonians 3:12. How does this verse describe the love we are supposed to have for one another? Our love should overflow to the people we know; and then, what does the verse say it should do?

• Our foam fountain went higher than we thought it would. How is that like the love that we are to have for one another? God wants us to love one another more than we even thought we could. The love we give should make people react the same way each of you did when you saw the foam fountain. God's love, shown through His people, should make people smile; it should make them want more. It should be something we want more of, just like we all wanted to see the fountain again.

Gel Us Together
Unity in the Church

Colossians 3:14 (NLT) - *And the most important piece of clothing you must wear is love. Love is what binds us all together in perfect harmony.*

Lab Equipment

- 10 oz Styrofoam™ cup
- 8 oz cup
- food coloring
- container of water (with food coloring in it)
- large spoon
- slush powder

Experiment

- Place one teaspoon of slush powder in the bottom of the 10 oz Styrofoam™ cup and set aside. (See appendix to order powder.)

- The children will name people in your congregation. Each time they name someone, they will add a spoonful of water to the 8 oz cup. Continue doing this until the cup is very full.

- The people we just named are all part of this church and important to it. Pour the water into the larger 10 oz cup that has the slush powder in it. (There is no need to stir it.)

- Talk briefly for 10-15 seconds, naming others that weren't named by the children.

- Then, turn the cup upside down and say, "The love we have for God and for one another is what holds us together." The children will gasp and then ooh-aah when the water does not pour out. It only takes a few seconds for the slush powder to join with the water to make a solid.

- Peel away the Styrofoam™ cup to reveal the jellied form.

44

Observation

• What were you expecting to happen when the cup was turned upside down?

• Touch the new solid and describe what it feels like.

• Name three differences in the water before and after it was poured into the new cup.

Discussion

• What did we put in the smaller cup? (spoonfuls of water) What did the spoonfuls of water represent? (people)

• What was added to the water when it was moved to the larger cup? (the powder) Something had to be added to it to make it hold together and form a solid.

• Read Colossians 3:14. What does bind mean? (hold together) What does this verse say is necessary to bind us or hold us together? (love) Whose love? (God's love and our love for one another) We are just a bunch of individual people, like all the spoonfuls of water. But, when love is added to those people–God's love and love for one another–they are held together. They are important to one another.

• How do people act toward each other when they bound together in love? What kinds of things do you see people who are bound together in love doing for one another? How do others know they are followers of God?

About slush powder:

• It can be added to most liquids to cause them to rapidly gel. Milk takes longer because of the fat content of the milk.

• Warmer liquids gel faster, but keep in mind they do not change temperature.

• It is biodegradable and can be disposed of under running water and through a garbage disposal.

• Although it is not toxic, slush powder should not be ingested. It is not a food product. If swallowed, drink lots of water. If it gets in eyes, flush them thoroughly.

Glow-in-the-Dark Name
All-Knowing God

Colossians 3:14 (NLT) -- *And the most important piece of clothing you must wear is love. Love is what binds us all together in perfect harmony.*

Lab Equipment

- black light
- craft brushes
- dye-free liquid detergent (Purex® works well)
- heavy black paper

Experiment

- Each child will write his or her name in BIG letters on the black paper. But they won't be using a traditional writing utensil. This time they will paint their name with the dye-free liquid detergent. Don't skimp on the detergent. The letters need to be thick.

- Children tend to write small even when given a large piece of paper. You may want to lightly write their names in pencil on the paper before they begin. This will give them a guideline to go by as they paint.

- Now, find something else to do for 45 minutes while the detergent dries.

- When the detergent is dry, turn out the lights and turn on the black light. Place the black paper in front of the black light. Cool! They can read their names even though the room is dark and the paper is black!

Observation

- What happened to the detergent under the black light?

- What happens if you turn out the lights but don't turn on the black light? Do the letters light up? Are they as bright?

- How many names were you able to read?

Discussion

- Do you think God knows about individual people or just what groups of people are doing? How much do you think He knows about you?

- Read Psalm 139:16. When did God start knowing you?

- What did you do today that God saw you do? What did you say today that God heard you say?

- Now read Psalm 139:1-4. What else does the Bible say that God knows about you?

- When we wrote our names, they weren't easy to read until we put them under the black light. Do you know the names of everyone in your city? Does anyone? God not only knows the names of everyone in your city, but also everyone in your state, in your country, and everyone in all the countries of the world. That's pretty amazing! When God looks at us, it's like a special light shines on us and He can see and know everything that is hidden.

- How do you feel when someone remembers your name? (It makes you feel special and important to that person.) God knows your name! You are special to Him. You are important to Him. He knows everything about you!

Hard Hearts
Unbelief

Hebrews 3:7-14 - *Today, if you hear his voice, do not harden your hearts as you did in the rebellion, during the time of testing in the desert, where your fathers tested and tried me and for forty years saw what I did. That is why I was angry with that generation, and I said, "Their hearts are always going astray, and they have not known my ways." So I declared on oath in my anger, "They shall never enter my rest."*

See to it, brothers, that none of you has a sinful, unbelieving heart that turns away from the living God. But encourage one another daily, as long as it is called Today, so that none of you may be hardened by sin's deceitfulness. We have come to share in Christ if we hold firmly till the end the confidence we had at first.

Lab Equipment

- 2 containers
- brown sugar
- one slice of fresh bread

Experiment

- Put ½ cup of brown sugar in each of two containers. Let both containers set out for several days so the brown sugar hardens.

- Place a piece of bread in one container. Seal both containers for a day.

- Look at and touch both samples of brown sugar.

- The brown sugar with the bread in it has softened, while the other container remained hard.

Observation

- What is the difference in the way the two containers of brown sugar look?

- What is the difference in the way the two containers of brown sugar feel?

- Which one of the containers had help to stay soft?

- The bread was very soft when it was put in the container. How does it feel now?

- Which brown sugar would you rather use?

Discussion

- Read Hebrews 3:7-14.

- What does it mean to have a hard heart? (When we say that someone has a hard heart, it means they don't display loving feelings.)

- What does it mean to have a hard heart against God? (When we sin against God, disobeying His Word, our hearts get hard; we no longer show God our love and we don't believe in His love. We shut ourselves off from Him by not believing and turning away from Him.)

- How did the bread help the one container?

- How can we keep our hearts from getting hard? (Verse 14 says we should hold firmly to God with confidence.)

- How can we help others not to have a hard heart? (We can encourage them to rely on God.)

- The bread helped the sugar stay soft. Verse 7 tells us who will help us keep our hearts from getting hard. Who is that? (The Holy Spirit.)

Hardly Shaking or Shaking Hard?

Anger

Proverbs 30:33 (NLT) - *As the beating of cream yields butter, and a blow to the nose causes bleeding, so anger causes quarrels.*

Lab Equipment

- clear glass quart jar with tight lid
- music
- paper towel
- pint of heavy cream
- salt
- saltine crackers
- small dish

Experiment

- Chill the heavy cream overnight. Pour it into the glass quart jar and tighten the lid.

- Hold the lid tightly in one hand and the bottom of the jar tightly in the other hand. Shake the jar HARD for 10-15 minutes.

- If you have a group working on this, start some praise music the kids can sing along with. One child will be shaking until you hit the pause button. The jar will pass to the next person, the music starts and the kids sing some more.

- When you start hearing and feeling a clump hit the sides, then it's just about ready. Shake hard for another 2 minutes.

- Pour as much of the water out of the jar as possible. Then, put the clump out on a heavy paper towel. Pat gently to absorb some more of the water.

- Add some salt and mash it into the butter to add more flavor. Serve to the kids on saltine crackers.

Observation

- What did the cream look like when you first put it in the jar?

- What did the watery substance that was poured off at the end look like?

- When you stuck a knife in the butter, what did it feel like? Was it hard or soft?

- What did the butter taste like?

Discussion

- Read Proverbs 30:33. Did you know that making butter was mentioned in the Bible? What does this verse say causes quarrels?

- When have you been angry about something and ended up arguing with someone? A quarrel is an argument. When we're angry, we're more likely to get into a bad quarrel.

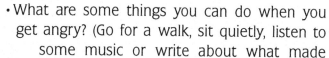

- What are some things you can do when you get angry? (Go for a walk, sit quietly, listen to some music or write about what made you angry.) Do you sometimes want to hit something? That's not a good idea. It ends up that you hurt yourself, you hurt someone else, or you break something. That's an irresponsible thing to do with your anger. The best thing to do is hold onto your tongue; watch your words. Wait until you calm down before you say anything. In anger we sometimes say things we really don't mean, because we're not thinking clearly. The anger is clogging up your brain. Maybe you should try making some butter!

I Don't Want to Be a Glob
Steadfast Belief

James 1:8 (NLT) – *They can't make up their minds. They waver back and forth in everything they do.*

Lab Equipment

- 2 small plastic cups
- Epsom Salt™
- paper towel
- plastic spoon
- tablespoon measure
- teaspoon measure
- water
- white glue
- Ziploc™ bag

Experiment

- Measure 1 tablespoon of white glue and put it in one of the plastic cups.

- In the other cup, put ½ teaspoon Epsom Salt™ and ½ teaspoon of warm water. Mix this thoroughly so the salt is completely dissolved.

- Add the salt mixture to the glue and mix.

- Pour the mixture from the cup onto the paper towel and pat it to squeeze out any extra water (it will appear very wet.)

- Kneed the glob, then place it in the palm of your hand and roll it into a ball.

- Drop the glob onto a hard surface and see what happens.

- When you're done playing, place the glob in the Ziploc™ bag to store.

Observation

- What happened when the glue and the Epsom Salt™ solution came together?

- Describe how the glob feels.

- What happened when the glob was dropped on the hard surface? What makes the glob fun to play with?

- Change the shape of the glob, so it isn't perfectly round. Now, drop it on the same surface. Did it bounce the same?

Discussion

- Name a time when you couldn't make a decision and went back and forth on what you wanted. When you were asked what you wanted for lunch, you said a hamburger, then you said chicken strips, and then you said a hamburger, and then you said chicken strips. You couldn't decide. It may be aggravating to your parents, but this kind of bouncing back and forth isn't a terrible thing.

- Read James 1:8 (NLT).

- Have you ever met anyone who couldn't decide what she believed? Maybe you know someone who says that lying is wrong, but then you hear him or her tell a lie. Maybe you know someone who says that stealing is wrong, but when they're in the checkout line, they sneak a package of gum in their pocket. These people can't decide what they really believe.

- What if someone asked you who you believe Jesus is? You say, "He's God's Son." Then, your friend says, "You don't really believe that, do you?" Then, you say, "Well, He was a really nice man." When it comes to our faith, what does James 1:8 tell us? We can't be bouncing back and forth.

- How can you connect our glob to James 1:8? (The glob bounces all over the place. If we don't really know what we believe, then we're spiritually like the glob, going from one belief to another.)

- Globs are fun to play with, but we don't want to be like one!

Leave an Impression
Love

John 13:35 (NLT)
Your love for one another will prove to the world that you are my disciples.

Lab Equipment

- a nice sunny day
- nature print paper (or blueprint paper)
- small objects

Experiment

- Tape a piece of the nature paper to the inside of a box lid. This activity is going to be done outside and you don't want a breeze to move it. Collect a few small objects from indoors, such as a key, coin, washer, safety pin, scissors, paper clamp, ring, macaroni, cookie cutter. Then, when the children are outdoors, they can collect some small objects from nature, such as a twig, flower, pine cone, leaf, and maybe even a bug.

- The children will choose some items and arrange them on their nature print paper. They may want to put them on the paper in a design or just choose an interesting assortment. Set the box lid in direct sunlight for 10 minutes. (Go play a game and enjoy yourself while the sun works on your picture!)

- Bring the box indoors and remove the objects.

- Follow the directions on the nature paper package and rinse the paper. If you are using blueprint paper, there is no need to rinse the paper.

- After just a few minutes, you will be able to tell what objects were on the paper, because their images were left.

Observation

- What did you think when the objects were removed from the paper?

- By looking at the prints left on the paper, name the objects that were sitting there. Look at someone else's creation and see if you can name what he put on his paper to sit in the sun.

- Did it take a short amount of time or a really long time to make the impression? Was it minutes or was it days?

Discussion

- We knew immediately what objects had been sitting on the paper when we pulled the objects away because the impression looked just like them. How do you think people describe you when you're not around?

- What kind of impressions can people leave? After meeting someone once, you may think he or she is really nice, shy, arrogant, generous, dedicated, etc.

- Read John 13:35. Jesus said there is something we can do that will leave an impression on the world. What does Jesus tell us to do? What do people think when they see us loving one another and loving people we don't know?

- Name three ways you can love the believers at your church. Now, name three ways you can love someone you don't know well.

- Do you want Jesus to make an impression on your life so that other people can identify you as a believer in Him? Even when you're not at church, do people know that Jesus has His mark on your life?

Led By a Cloud
Israelites in the Desert

Exodus 13:20-22 (NLT) – Leaving Succoth, they camped at Etham on the edge of the wilderness. The Lord guided them by a pillar of cloud during the day and a pillar of fire at night. That way they could travel whether it was day or night. And the Lord did not remove the pillar of cloud or pillar of fire from their sight.

Lab Equipment

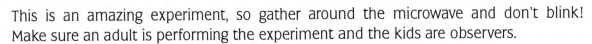

- bar of Ivory® soap
- large paper plate
- microwave oven

Experiment

This is an amazing experiment, so gather around the microwave and don't blink! Make sure an adult is performing the experiment and the kids are observers.

- Not just any soap will work; you need Ivory®.

- Unwrap a bar of Ivory® soap and place it in the center of a large sturdy paper plate. Put the plate in the center of the microwave oven and cook on HIGH for about 2 minutes. Within 10 seconds you'll start to see things change. Be careful not to leave it in the oven too long. If the soap starts touching the sides of the microwave, you'll want to stop. You don't enjoy popcorn that's been overcooked, and you certainly don't want to burn your soap!

- Remove it from the microwave and let it cool for another 2 minutes.

- You've created an amazing soapy cloud!

Observation

- What do you expect the soap to feel like now? (After guessing, let the children gently touch the soap.) Were you surprised?

- In its new form, what does it remind you of? (a cloud)

- Break off a piece and see if it still works like soap. Even though we wouldn't think it was a bar of soap if we saw it sitting on the counter, it does exactly what we expect soap to do.

Discussion

- In the book of Exodus the Bible tells us about the Israelites who left Egypt, where they were slaves, to go to the Promised Land. God led them out of Egypt, but because of their disobedience, God led them around the desert for 40 years instead of taking them directly to the Promised Land.

- How did God lead them? Read Exodus 13:20-22. (He led them with a cloud during the day and a pillar of fire at night.)

- Why did God lead them in two different ways? (During the day the Israelites could see a cloud, but at night they couldn't. At night they could easily see a pillar of fire but not a cloud.)

- How was our experiment with the soap like this story? (The Ivory® soap changed the way it looked to us, but it was still soap. God changed the way He appeared to the Israelites, but it was still God leading them.)

- Have you ever felt God leading you? What made you think it was God directing you? Have you ever come across a verse and it was just what you needed that day? Or, someone said something to you that helped you make a decision? Or, when you prayed about something you knew what you should do? (God leads His people through the Scriptures, through other believers, and through prayer.) What other ways does He lead us?

Clean-Up

Scrub the inside of the microwave thoroughly, then leave it standing open to air. Ivory® soap has a strong smell and you don't want your next helping of mashed potatoes to taste like soap!

Other stories to use this experiment with:

- Ascension (Luke 24:50-51)
- Elijah and the little cloud (1 Kings 18:44)
- The transfiguration (Luke 9:28–36)

Lighten the Load
His Burden Is Light

Matthew 11:30 (NLT) – *For my yoke fits perfectly, and the burden I give you is light.*

Lab Equipment

- 2 clear plastic cups
- 2 large metal washers
- 3 pieces of string
  (each 10" in length)
- plastic ruler that has a hole
  in the center
- water

TRY TO STAY "LEVEL-HEADED" FOR THIS ONE!

Experiment

- Tie one piece of string around the ruler
  at the ½" mark.

- Tie a second piece of string around
  the ruler at the 11½" mark.

- Tie a metal washer to the free end of each of these
  pieces of string.

- Tie the third piece of string through the center hole of the ruler. This will be the string
  that you hold onto.

- Hold onto this center string and observe how the washers are hanging. You want to
  create a balance, so if it is not hanging in balance, move the end strings toward the
  middle or closer to the end until it is in balance.

- Set the cups 11" from one another and fill them to the rim.

- Lower the ruler so that one of the washers goes into one of the cups. The ruler will
  no longer be in balance.

- Now, lower the ruler so that both washers go in the water, and you're back
  to being balanced.

Observation

- What happened when one washer was dipped into the water? How did it affect the other washer? Did it feel different in your hand?

- What happened when you dipped both washers into the water? Did it change the way it felt as you were holding it? How?

- What happened to the water when the washers were put in it?

Discussion

- A yoke is a piece of wood that is fitted over a person's shoulders to help carry buckets. One bucket hangs on each end and is balanced by the other. Using a yoke makes it easier to carry large buckets of water or containers of grain, but you can put anything you need to carry in the buckets. A yoke can also be used on an animal.

- How is what we created in our experiment like a yoke?

- What we do in our lives when we are within God's plan is easier because He is with us. If we try to do it on our own, it's like we're trying to carry two huge buckets without using a yoke.

Make It Float
Baby Moses in the Nile River

Exodus 1:6-2:10

Lab Equipment

- 2 balloons
- 2 Ziploc™ bags
- craft sticks
- items that will sink (rock, key, golf ball, dime, spoon, screw)
- large pan of water
- packing tape
- plastic spoon

Experiment

- Give the children one item at a time that you already know will sink, such as a rock, key, golf ball, dime, spoon or screw. Drop them in the water and watch them sink. Then, retrieve the items from the pan of water.

- Present the children with all the other objects you have collected from the Lab Equipment list. Using any or all of these items, they will figure out different methods of getting the items that previously sank to now float. (The more children, the more of these supplies you will need. Make sure they have plenty of supplies to experiment with.)

Observation

- The children will share the wild and crazy methods they created for making the sinking items now float.

- Which ones successfully floated, even when one of the objects known to sink were on board?

- After seeing each other's projects, are there modifications that the groups want to make?

Discussion

Pharaoh was the ruler of Egypt where the Israelites were slaves. The Egyptians treated Pharaoh as a god and didn't question anything he said. But, the Israelites worshipped God Almighty, the one true God. When Pharaoh realized that the Israelites were having more and more children, he was afraid that soon they would outnumber the Egyptians and take over the land. So, he made a new law that all the Israelite baby boys should be killed.

Jachobed was an Israelite mother who had a baby boy and two older children. She couldn't bear the thought of her little boy being killed, so she did her best to hide him for three months. That was very difficult to do! Babies cry and make all kinds of baby noises when you don't expect it. But Jachobed came up with a plan to protect her baby boy. She made a basket to put the baby in, and then she was going to place it in the river. But the basket would sink when the water came in between the papyrus weaving. She came up with another plan. She would seal it with tar and pitch to make it waterproof.

With the baby in the basket, Jachobed and her daughter, Miriam, went to the Nile River where they placed the basket in the grasses at the water's edge. Jachobed went home, but Miriam stayed behind to watch the basket. Soon, the Pharaoh's daughter came to the river to bathe and discovered the basket. When she opened it, she found the baby there. Even though she knew it was an Israelite baby boy, she wanted to keep the baby and protect him. Miriam quickly came out of hiding and went up to the princess. She offered to find someone to care for the baby for her. The princess thought that was a wonderful idea! So, Miriam went to get her mother. When Jachobed came back to the river with Miriam, the princess offered to pay her to take care of the baby until he was old enough to come live at the palace. The princess called the baby Moses because that means "drawn out of the water."

- What did Jachobed have to make float?

- How did Jachobed keep the baby Moses and the basket from sinking? There are many ways that you can make an object float and Jachobed came up with a good way to keep baby Moses floating.

- Describe tar and pitch. How did they keep the basket from sinking?

- What do you admire about Jachobed? What do you admire about Miriam?

Melting Ice
Salt of the Earth

Matthew 5:13 (NIV) - *You are the salt of the earth. But if the salt loses its saltiness, how can it be made salty again? It is no longer good for anything, except to be thrown out and trampled by men.*

Lab Equipment

- 2 bowls for each child
- 2 ice cubes for each child
- salt shaker

Experiment

- The children will place one ice cube in each bowl. Generously shake salt on one of the ice cubes and then set both aside for 5 minutes.

- The ice cube that had salt sprinkled on it will be much more melted than the one without the salt.

Observation

After 5 minutes, observe what has happened to the ice cubes.

- How are they different now?

- Which one melted faster?

- What caused one to melt faster than the other?

Discussion

• What are some of the things that salt is used for? (to flavor food, to preserve meat, as an antiseptic, to light fires, to create thirst and to melt ice)

• Read Matthew 5:13.

• Think about the uses of salt. When Jesus said that we were to be the salt of the earth, what do you think He meant? (Revisit each one of the uses they came up with for salt.)

  • We are to make the world better by flavoring it with God's love.

  • We should keep the world from getting rotten by trying to keep it from decaying with sin. We should try to preserve our belief in Jesus.

  • Salt pulls out infection and we should help pull out the infection of sin that is in the world by introducing people to Jesus.

  • When you throw salt on a fire, the flames go higher. Sometimes we think of the Spirit of God as a flame inside us, and if we are supposed to be the salt of the earth, that flame should go higher and burn brighter.

• By being around us and seeing how God lives in us, people should want the same thing; seeing us should make them thirsty for God.

• Describe ice. It's cold and hard. Some people have hearts that are cold and hard. They are unkind and don't want to live by God's Word. When they see God alive in us, their hearts should be softened and warmed up to God. They should melt like the salt melts the ice.

Mighty Puffs
Power & Obedience

Psalm 148:7-8 (NLT) - *Praise the Lord from the earth, you creatures of the ocean depths, fire and hail, snow and storm, wind and weather that obey him.*

Lab Equipment

• Airzooka (See "Supply Sites" to order this)
• match
• paper cup
• votive candle

Experiment

• Before using the Airzooka in front of the kids, practice and figure out how to aim. There is a sight guide on the Airzooka, and once you become familiar with it, aiming is easy. Pull back on the button attached to the elastic and a giant puff of air is in your control.

• Start by blowing a puff of air at the children. Make sure you hit them on different parts of their body.

• Then, set a paper cup on someone's head. Stand back 8-10 feet and pluck the Airzooka. You will be able to knock the cup off the child's head.

• After doing this to several children, move on to blowing out a candle. Set the candle on a table and light it. Stand back 8 feet and see if you can blow out the candle.

• Every time you are successful at extinguishing the flame, relight the candle and increase the distance by a foot.

• Return to an 8-foot distance. Ask someone to stand between you and the candle and slightly out of the Airzooka line of fire. When the Airzooka is released, this person will try to interrupt the wind blast with their hand, before it reaches the flame.

Observation

• How did the Airzooka feel when it hit you?

• What happened to the cup?

• What happened to the candle?

• Could you see the air coming out of the Airzooka? Could you see what blew out the candle?

• Who had control of what the Airzooka did?

Discussion

• Read Psalm 148:7-8. In this verse, what obeys God? The air blast from the Airzooka was under the control of whoever was holding it, but the winds are much greater than what the Airzooka can do. God can tell the winds when to blow, where to blow, and how hard to blow. Can you think of a story in the Bible when the weather obeyed God? When Jesus and His disciples were out in a boat, a storm came up. The disciples feared for their lives but Jesus commanded the storm to calm down and the water and winds immediately became calm.

• Now read more of the same Psalm. Read Psalm 148:9-14. This Psalm praises God for His mighty power over everything on the earth. What other things does it name that obey God? (They are all under His control. He is the Creator and all His creation should praise Him!)

• What does God ask of us? (Just as the winds and the weather, the mountains and animals, He wants us to obey Him and praise Him.)

Milk Kaleidoscope
God's Plan

Jeremiah 29:11 (NLT) - *For I know the plans I have for you, says the Lord. They are plans for good and not for disaster, to give you a future and a hope.*

Lab Equipment

- food coloring
- liquid detergent (Dawn® works well)
- pie pan
- whole milk

Experiment

- Fill the pie pan about halfway with the whole milk.

- Gently squeeze drops of different colors of food coloring into the milk. Put at least 20 drops.

- Drizzle the liquid detergent onto the surface of the milk around the edge of the pan and watch.

- The surface tension has been disrupted and the colors explode into beautiful rings.

Observation

- What did the drops of food coloring do when you first put them in the milk?

- When the liquid detergent was added to the milk, what happened to the drops of food coloring?

- What words would you use to describe the colors once you added the liquid detergent?

Discussion

- The liquid detergent disturbed the surface tension and made it possible for the food coloring to be released into the milk.

- Each child will write down 3 things they see themselves doing in 20 years. Actually add 20 to the children's ages, and tell them someone they know who is that age. Take time to share what the children wrote down.

- Read Jeremiah 29:11. You just shared some possibilities for your life, but what does this verse say? It says that God has a plan for your life. It's not just a good plan either; it's the best plan! His plan may surprise you. It may be something you never imagined yourself doing. No matter what it is, you can know that when God created you, He created you with a very special plan in mind that is all yours.

- Ask someone to share with the children where God is leading them and how it may have been something unexpected. How have they realized it was a good plan?

- The liquid detergent caused the food coloring to explode into something unexpected and beautiful. There was much more there than we thought. The different drops moved toward one another and swirled together. When we give ourselves to God, asking Him to show us the special plan He has in mind for us, He will cause something unexpected and beautiful to explode in you. Life will be much more than you ever anticipated!

- Think of each drop of coloring as someone in this world. People are all different colors. God has a plan for each person in this world and each time someone discovers something about his or her personal plan, God makes life more exciting. Can you imagine what the world would be like if everyone were living in God's plan for them?

67

Mirror, Mirror, on the Wall
Reflections of God's Glory

2 Corinthians 3:18 (NLT) - *And all of us have had that veil removed so that we can be mirrors that brightly reflect the glory of the Lord. And as the Spirit of the Lord works within us, we become more and more like him and reflect his glory even more.*

Lab Equipment

- 3 rectangular mirrors the same size
- different color of tiny pieces of paper or aquarium rocks
- drinking straws
- masking tape

Experiment

- Do this experiment in a well-lit area. On a sturdy surface, stand the three mirrors on one of their edges and lean them against one another for support to form a triangle. The mirrored sides should be facing the inside of the triangle.

- Attach the mirrors to each other by applying masking tape down each of the seams, on the backside of the mirrors.

- Place one little piece of colored paper in the center of the triangle.

- Now, put several different colors of paper in the center of the triangle.

- Move the pieces of paper around with a drinking straw. You've made your own kaleidoscope of colors.

Observation

- How many times could you see the one object when it was the only thing in the center?

- What did you see when you added more pieces of paper?

- What happened when you moved the pieces around?

- Which way was the prettiest? Which way was more exciting?

- Look at the mirrors from a different position. Do you see the same thing? Are there more or fewer pieces?

Discussion

- When you look in a mirror, you see one of yourself. What is that called? (reflection)

- Why did we see more than one of the pieces of paper when we put them in the middle of the mirrors? (They reflected off one another and just kept going.) The image that was reflected by one mirror was reflected into a different mirror, which was reflected again, and so on and so on.

- As the placement of the papers was changed with the straw, what happened to the pattern? How many different patterns do you think could be created?

- Read 2 Corinthians 3:18. Who does this scripture call a "mirror"? Why are we called mirrors? What is it that we are to reflect?

- How would you describe God's glory?

- How can we reflect God's glory? (The number of ways we can do that is endless, just like the reflections of the papers were too many to count.)

- How much are we to reflect God's glory?

- God wants us to be His mirrors, reflecting His beautiful glory in everything we do. What one way can you be a better mirror for God this week?

Mysterious Movement
Understanding

Hebrews 6:3 (NLT) - And so, God willing, we will move forward to further understanding.

Lab Equipment

- magnet
- metal cookie sheet
- small metal objects
- small plastic objects

Experiment

- Arrange the small metal and plastic objects along one end of the cookie sheet.

- Place a magnet underneath one of the objects on the cookie sheet. Slowly move the magnet down the cookie sheet. Some of the objects will move and some will not. Determine which objects will move with the magnet's guidance.

Observation

- Which objects did not move?

- Which objects moved down the cookie sheet?

- Find another object that you think would not move and another object that you think would move. Place them on the cookie sheet and see if you are correct.

Discussion

- Read Hebrews 6:3. What does God want us to move toward? One of our goals should be better understanding. But what are we trying to understand?

- How do the cookie sheet, magnets, and objects remind you of this verse?

- What can we do to gain better understanding of God?

- Are there people who understand everything about God? (No.) Who is this verse written to? (Everyone!) We all need to keep moving forward to better understand the God who created everything.

- Name three things that you would like to understand better about God. How will you move toward that? Who will you ask to help you understand?

- How do you feel when you haven't learned anything in a long time? How do you feel when you learn something new? It's exciting when the light bulb comes on and you can see the answers to your questions! God does not get mad when we ask questions. He wants us to come to a better understanding, so don't be afraid to ask questions.

No Leaks
Troubles

Isaiah 43:2 (NLT) - When you go through deep waters and great trouble, I will be with you. When you go through rivers of difficulty, you will not drown! When you walk through the fire of oppression, you will not be burned up; the flames will not consume you.

Lab Equipment

- 3 round pencils (very important that they be round)
- small Ziploc® bag
- towel paper
- water

Experiment

- Sharpen three round pencils. The pencils should be sharpened to a fine point. Do not use pencils with edges.

- Fill the Ziploc® bag about half full with water and seal it completely.

- Grip the top of the bag firmly and hold a pencil in the other hand.

- What do you think will happen if a pencil is poked through the bag? Let's find out. Push the pencil through one side of the bag and out the other side. The bag will seal itself around the pencil and there shouldn't be any water spilled. Whew! One worked. Now, push the other two pencils through the bag.

- Move to the sink when removing the pencils from the bag.

Observation

- What was the expression on the onlookers' faces when the pencil started through the bag?

- How much water came out of the bag when the pencil was poked through?

- Was it difficult to get the pencil through the bag?

- What would happen if you pushed the pencils all the way through the bag and all the way out the other side?

- Try the experiment with pencils that have edges or with a heavier bag. What do you think will happen?

Discussion

- The Ziploc® bag is a little stretchy. Each time a hole was poked in the bag, it stretched closer to the pencil and prevented the bag from leaking. The round edges and the sharp tip of the pencil protected us from getting wet!

- Read Isaiah 43:2. What does this verse say to you? God tells us through this verse that no matter what we go through, no matter how terrible we think a problem is, He will go through it with us. He also tells us that we won't drown. Our troubles won't win. And no matter how many things scare us, like the pencils going through the bag, God will be there with us.

- This verse calls our troubles "deep waters." When you're in deep water and you can't swim well, it can be really frightening. But, if someone who is a great swimmer is with you and can help you back to safety, then you're not as scared. You know you're in good hands.

- Name some troubles that you, your family, or a friend of yours has had. Have you asked God to go with you through this "deep water"? How does that make a difference in the way you feel about your troubles?

- Ask an adult to share with you how God has helped them through some of their personal "deep waters."

Now You See Him, Now You Don't
Jesus Appears and Disappears

Luke 24:13-16, 31 (NLT) - *That same day two of Jesus' followers were walking to the village of Emmaus, seven miles out of Jerusalem. As they walked along they were talking about everything that had happened. Suddenly, Jesus himself came along and joined them and began walking beside them. But they didn't know who he was, because God kept them from recognizing him. ... Suddenly, their eyes were opened, and they recognized him. And at that moment he disappeared!*

Lab Equipment

- ammonia
- cotton balls
- goldenrod paper (just the color, goldenrod, not a special type of paper)
- vinegar
- water
- white taper candle

Storytelling

Make sure you get real goldenrod paper and not just a bright yellow. Use this experiment to actually be part of the telling of the story of the stranger on the Road to Emmaus. Before beginning, write "JESUS" in large letters on the goldenrod paper using the white candle. Make the letters wide and then brush away any excess wax.

Read Luke 24:13-14. Dip a cotton ball in some ammonia water and squeeze out the excess. Wipe the cotton ball across the paper from side-to-side, working your way down the paper. The paper will turn a reddish color and the letters of "JESUS" will appear.

When the children stop their ooohs and aaahs, continue reading the Luke 24:15-16 and 31a. Pause for a moment before finishing verse 31. Dip a different cotton ball in some vinegar and squeeze out the excess. As you say the last of that verse, "And at that moment He disappeared!" wipe across the paper again. This time the paper will return to its original color and you will no longer be able to see the letters written there.

Discussion

- How do you think the two men felt when they realized it was Jesus they were walking with?

- What did you think when JESUS appeared on the paper?

- How do you think the men felt when Jesus disappeared as quickly as He had appeared?

- What did you think when the paper returned to its original color?

- The children may want you to do it again, so use that as part of the lesson. It was exciting to have Jesus with them, and they surely wanted Him to appear to them again!

- Now, give everyone their very own paper and candle to try the same experiment.

Our Center of Gravity
Riches

Psalm 62:10 (NLT) - *If your wealth increases, don't make it the center of your life.*

Lab Equipment

- 2 drinking straws
- black permanent marker
- CD case
- small piece of play dough

Experiment

- Stand a CD case on end. You will need to hold onto it to make sure it stays steady during this experiment.

- Lay one of the drinking straws across the edge of the CD case until it is balanced and will stay by itself. Put a mark on the straw at the point where it is resting on the CD case.

- Place a very small amount of play dough around the end of the other drinking straw.

- Lay the second drinking straw with the play dough on it across the edge of the CD case until it is also balanced. Make a mark on this straw at the point where it touches the CD case.

Observation

- Describe where the first straw is resting on the CD case. Measure from each end of the straw to the mark made by the black marker. How do these measurements compare?

- Describe where the second straw touches the CD case. Did the second straw rest about the same place as the first straw? Was it easier or more difficult to figure out where it should rest on the CD case?

- Add more play dough to the second straw and see what happens.

Discussion

- We found the center of gravity of each straw and marked it with the marker. The center of gravity is where something can rest and be balanced.

- Read Psalm 62:10.

- Compare this verse to our experiment. What represents the center of our lives? (the mark made on the straws) What does the play dough represent? (our riches being important)

- What happened to the center of your life when riches became important? (became heavier, the center of our life moved) What did the center of your life move closer to? (the riches) Riches became more important than they should have and your life changed how it was balanced.

- What should the center of our lives be? (our relationship with God) Other things, like our money, shouldn't become so important that they push God out of the center.

- Read Psalm 62:10 again. The verse doesn't say that having money is bad, but it does say that we have to be careful not to make money the center of our lives.

TRY BALANCING THE STRAWS ON YOUR FINGER, TOO!

Passing the Word
Evangelism

Acts 16:32 (NLT) - *Then they shared the word of the Lord with him and all who lived in his household.*

Lab Equipment

- 6 marbles
- book

Experiment

- Open the book to approximately the halfway point and lay it on a table.

- Place 5 of the marbles in the binding crease of the book.

- Set the sixth marble at the edge of the binding crease.

- Flick the sixth marble with your finger to propel it into the other marbles. You want it to strike the other marbles with as much force as possible. If you can't flick very well (like me!) then use a small dowel rod, something like a pool cue, to hit the marble.

- The marble at the other end will roll down the binding.

Observation

- What happened when the first ball made contact with the set of marbles?

- Flick the marble with different amounts of force. Does that affect what happens to the other marbles?

Discussion

- Read the story of Paul and Silas in jail from Acts 16:16-34.

- What was the first thing that happened? (In the name of Jesus, Paul commanded the demon out of the slave girl.) What happened next? And next? Continue asking for the main points throughout the story.

- It all started when Paul and Silas encountered the slave girl. Because of their actions, the jailer became a believer in Jesus. But, what happened after that? (The jailer's entire household became believers.)

- How is this like what happened to the marbles?

- How can you pass on the word about who Jesus is? Who can you tell about Jesus?

- We may never know what happens when we tell someone about Jesus. They may tell someone else, who tells someone else, who tells someone else. The reaction continues and the message of Jesus is spread.

Potato Plunge
God Will Never Leave Us

Nehemiah 9:31 (NLT) - *But in your great mercy, you did not destroy them completely or abandon them forever. What a gracious and merciful God you are!*

Lab Equipment

- clear glass mixing bowl
- pie tin
- small plastic glass that has a flat bottom
- small potato

Experiment

- Place the glass mixing bowl on the table with the pie tin sitting on top of it.

- Turn the plastic glass upside down in the center of the pie tin and set the potato on top of it.

- Grip the pie tin securely and yank it quickly. Both the small plastic glass and the pie tin will pull toward you. The potato, though, should fall into the bowl.

Observation

- What did you expect to happen?

- What did you notice about the pie tin and the bowl?

- What did you notice about the potato when the pie tin was yanked?

Discussion

- All of a sudden the pie tin and the small glass were no longer there to support the potato. If the bowl had not been there, what would have happened to the potato?

- Has there been a time in your life when a friend or family member was no longer there to support you? Tell about that time. Who did you turn to?

- Draw similarities between the potato (you), the bowl (God), the pie tin and glass (friends and family). When others disappoint us or aren't there when we'd like for them to be, God will not abandon us. He will always be there.

- Sometimes people say they've had "the rug pulled out from under them." What would happen if someone pulled the rug you were standing on out from under you? (You'd fall to the ground.) Would anyone be there to catch you? (just the hard floor) When people say that, they don't mean a real rug has been pulled out from under them, but that they were surprised when things changed and they could no longer depend on who or what they thought they could. No matter what people do to us, God is there and we can depend on Him.

- Read Nehemiah 9:31 and be glad that God will never abandon us!

Praying Hands
Prayer

James 5:16 (NLT) - Confess your sins to each other and pray for each other so that you may be healed. The earnest prayer of a righteous person has great power and wonderful results.

Lab Equipment

- Magnet Wand (See "Supply Sites" to order this)
- paper clip

Experiment

- Place the paper clip on a flat surface. Cover it with your hand. Make sure your hand is flat against the surface and that the paper clip is under your palm.

- Position the magnet against the back of your hand. Slowly raise your hand, keeping the magnet against your skin.

- The paper clip will hang from the palm of your hand.

- Keeping the magnet against the back of your hand, move your hand slowly in circles.

Observation

- When you had the paper clip on the table by itself, what was it doing? Lay the paper clip on the surface by itself to clarify.

- When you positioned the magnet and raised your hand, what did the paper clip do?

- When you moved your hand around what did the paper clip do?

Discussion

- Read James 5:16. What are we supposed to do for one another? (pray for each other)

- Go through the experiment again, using one of the children's hands this time, explaining as you go. If the paper clip is someone you know who never wants to talk about the Lord, or someone who is lonely or has hurt feelings, or someone who is ill, what does this verse tell us to do? We need to cover them with prayer. (Place your hand over the paper clip.)

- If we think of the magnet as God (position it on the back of your hand), then God can work through our prayers. There are wonderful results when we pray for others. Share a time when you have prayed for someone and were amazed at what happened.

- Do we have to wait until our special prayer time to pray for them? When we cover someone in prayer that means that we pray for them constantly, no matter what we're doing throughout the day. Just like the paper clip hung on when our hand moved from place to place, our prayers can help others hang on to God.

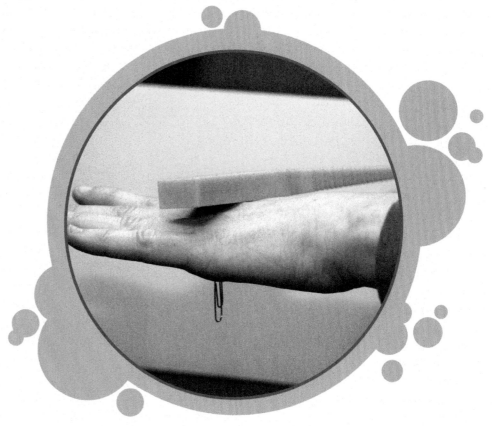

Raisin' and Praisin'
Praise

Psalm 116:13 (NLT) – *I will lift up a cup symbolizing his salvation; I will praise the Lord's name for saving me.*

Psalm 25:1 (NLT) – *To you, O Lord, I lift up my soul.*

Psalm 123:1 (NLT) – *I lift my eyes to you, O God, enthroned in heaven.*

Lab Equipment

- deflated balloon
- mug

Experiment

- Place the cup and the balloon on the table. Ask the children to try to pick up the cup without touching it with their hands.

- When they are dismayed because it's impossible to pick up the cup without touching it, hold the balloon by the neck so that most of the balloon is dangling inside the mug.

- Blow the balloon up until it is firmly lodged in the mug. Clasp the neck of the balloon securely so the air won't escape, and the mug can then be lifted off the table.

Observation

- Describe what you saw. What was lifting the mug?

- Is the balloon sticky? Is that what is causing it to stay in the mug?

- What would happen if you started letting a little bit of air out of the balloon?

- Can you think of anything else you could lift up using this method?

Discussion

- Name some things that you can lift high. (book, finger, ball)

- Look up Psalm 116:13, Psalm 25:1 and Psalm 123:1. Tell what is being lifted high in each one of these verses. What does it say the cup is representing? God's salvation fills us, like something filling a cup. In praise to God, the writer of the Psalm is lifting up his salvation, his soul and his eyes. Try to describe the feelings of the Psalm writer as he wrote these verses.

- What else can you lift up in praise to God? (lift your voice, lift your song, lift your hands)

- Try writing your own psalm of praise using the words "lift up."

Rising to the Top
Overcoming

Isaiah 43:2 (NLT) - When you go through deep waters and great trouble, I will be with you. When you go through rivers of difficulty, you will not drown! When you walk through the fire of oppression, you will not be burned up; the flames will not consume you.

Lab Equipment

- corn meal
- empty jar (peanut butter or canning jar)
- large marble

Experiment

- Give each child an empty jar, a large marble and access to a supply of corn meal.

- Place the marble in the jar. This marble represents you.

- Name one thing that gets you down. Then pour ¼ cup of corn meal into the jar on top of the marble. Continue to name things that get you down and add the ¼ cup of corn meal each time until the jar is about two-thirds the way full. Point out that there is a lot of corn meal on top of the marble and that there seems to be a lot of difficult, troubling times on top of you.

- Put the lid on securely. Shake the jar in a circular forward motion. (Try this beforehand so you can demonstrate to the children.) As the children are shaking, loudly and enthusiastically say things like, "I'm relying on God to get me through...(and finish the sentence with one of the troubling times the kids have shared)!" "God will never leave me!" "God can lift me out of my sad times!"

- After just a few shakes the marble will rise and sit on top of the cornmeal.

Observation

• Where did the marble start out?

• Where was the marble when you stopped?

• Was the jar ever opened after the marble went in?

• What did you do to make the marble come to the top?

Discussion

• What did you expect to happen?

• Every time you shook the jar, a little bit of the corn meal moved underneath the marble and raised it up. Before it could get covered up with the corn meal again the corn meal moved beneath it. Eventually, the marble was sitting on top of the corn meal.

• Read Isaiah 43:10. How does this verse make you feel?

• How is this like God helping us through difficult times? (Sometimes we feel like our world is being shaken and everything is coming down on top of us.) When we rely on God for our strength and comfort, He will help us stay on top of the frustrating, sad and scary times in our lives. Depending on God will keep us from feeling smothered when we don't know how we'll ever recover.

Rolling Forward
Understanding

Hebrews 6:3 (NLT) - *And so, God willing, we will move forward to further understanding.*

Lab Equipment

- 12, foot-long dowel rods (any diameter as long as they are the same)
- a box full of books

Experiment

- Place the box of books on the table. Each child will use one finger to push the box down the table. They will probably be able to move it, but keep in mind how difficult or easy it was to do.

- Lay the dowel rods on the table, parallel and 2-3 inches from one another. Set the box on top of the dowel rods.

- Once again, each child will use one finger to push the box down the table. As the box rolls along, one dowel rod at a time will be exposed. Pick it up and place it in front of the box so the box will continue to roll.

Observation

- What was the difference between the ways we tried to move the box?

- Was it easier to move the box using the dowel rods or without them?

- Which way would you rather move the box? Why? Which way would help you take the box of books further?

Discussion

• Have you ever memorized a scripture but didn't know what it really meant? What makes it easier to remember a scripture for a long time? (when you understand it, when you use it, when you know what it means in your life)

• Read Hebrews 6:3. What do you think this verse means?

• If the box of books in our experiment represents God's Word, the Bible, then what would the dowel rods represent? (our understanding) When we come to church, read our Bibles and pray, then our life with God moves forward and we grow closer to Him. As we understand and learn, God becomes a bigger part of our lives.

• What can you do that will help you understand scriptures better? Do you understand scriptures better when you make a tune to go with a verse? Does drawing help you remember God's Word better? Maybe the more you read, the more you remember. You might need to ask other people what the scripture means to them. The important thing is that you keep moving ahead in understanding. God will help you!

Satan Crusher
Power over Satan

Romans 16:20 (NLT) - *The God of peace will soon crush Satan under your feet. May the grace of our Lord Jesus Christ be with you.*

Lab Equipment

- crushed ice
- empty pop can (preferably Orange Crush™ or another Crush™ flavor)
- large bowl
- portable electric burner
- tongs
- water

Experiment

- If you have access to a kitchen, gather the children where they can see the stove; otherwise, use a portable electric burner.

- Fill the large bowl about two-thirds with ice.

- Put about 2 tablespoons of water in the bottom of the pop can. Set it on the burner and heat it until you see steam coming from the pull tab opening.

- Use the tongs to remove the can from the burner, placing it immediately down into the ice. DON'T TOUCH THE CAN. Something will happen within a few seconds.

- There will be a pop and the can will be crushed...and no one touched it!

Observation

- What did you hear?

- What happened to the can when it was pushed into the ice?

- How far was the can down in the ice?

Discussion

- Are there some people that Satan doesn't bother with? When we become a Christian, does Satan run and hide?

- What kind of trouble does Satan put in our way?

- When do you think Satan attacks most?

- Tell about a time when you felt like Satan was at work.

- How can you recognize that something is Satan's work?

  Ask yourself if this is something that would please God. If it isn't, then it's Satan working. Know your Bible well. Then, when you have questions, you will know what God's Word says. When you're unsure, talk to one of your spiritual leaders–someone you respect because they put God first in their lives.

- Read Romans 16:20. What does this verse say that God will do to Satan?

  The can got very hot, but when we placed it in the ice, it collapsed. It was crushed; it didn't have a chance. Satan doesn't have a chance against our all-powerful God. God will crush him!

Sin Trap
Escaping Sin

Proverbs 29:6 (NLT) - *Evil people are trapped by sin, but the righteous escape, shouting for joy.*

Lab Equipment

- 2 identical glass jars
- 4" x 4" piece of cardstock
- match
- twine

Experiment

- Place one jar in the freezer for 5 minutes. Put the other jar in a sink of very hot water for the same amount of time. Remove the jars and dry them thoroughly.

- Stand the jars on top of one another, mouth-to-mouth, with the index card between them and the warm jar on the bottom.

- Light the end of the twine. When it begins to smoke, lift the index card and top cold jar, keeping the card against the mouth of the jar. Dangle the smoking end of the twine into the bottom jar and close the opening by bringing the card and jar back down. Don't let go, because the twine sticking out causes the jars to be unstable. When the bottom jar fills with smoke, remove the twine and the index card, resting the cold top jar on the warm bottom jar. Watch where the smoke goes.

- Do the same experiment, only this time the warm jar will go on the top and the cold jar will be on the bottom. Put the twine in the bottom jar, which is the cold jar this time. Watch where the smoke goes.

Observation

• In which trial did the smoke move around the jars freely? Which jar was on the bottom?

• In which trial was the smoke trapped in the bottom jar? Which jar was on the bottom?

Discussion

• Read Proverbs 29:6.

• Which experiment was like the evil people who are trapped by sin? Which experiment was like the righteous who escape?

• What does this verse mean—being trapped by sin? How does sin trap people?

• What does it mean to be righteous? Why do the righteous shout for joy?

• Have you ever done something that you know didn't please God, but you didn't know how to make it right or how to stop doing it again? Lying is like that. You tell one lie, and then when someone questions you about it, you tell another lie, which leads to another and another. That's a sin trap! Can you name any other sin traps?

Spirit-Filled Rockets
God Sends Us

Acts 1:8 (NLT) - But when the Holy Spirit has come upon you, you will receive power and will tell people about me everywhere—in Jerusalem, throughout Judea, in Samaria, and to the ends of the earth.

Lab Equipment

- Alka-Seltzer® tablet
- cardboard roll from paper towel
- duct tape (or packing tape)
- Fuji™ brand film canister (clear)
- small piece of aluminum foil
- warm water

Experiment

- Cover one end of the cardboard tube with a small piece of aluminum foil. Then duct tape it securely in place by going across the end and around the tube. You want to close off the end of the tube but not have the sticky side of the tape exposed inside the tube.

- Fill the film canister halfway with warm water. Prepare and rehearse the rest of the steps, so you can do them quickly. The reaction will not wait until you're ready!

- Break the Alka-Seltzer® tablet in 3 or 4 pieces. Drop one piece into the film canister and snap on the lid.

- Insert the film canister into the cardboard tube, lid first, and let it slide to the covered end.

- Point the open end of the cardboard tube up and away from you.

- When the canister flies out of the cardboard tube, it will probably leave the lid and part of the liquid in the tube. Dump that out immediately so your tube can be reused.

- Do this several times and mark where the canisters land. Measure the distance from where they launched to the landing point.

Observation

- What happened that made the canisters fly through the air?

- How far did the canisters go?

- Were some of the film canisters closer than others? Change the temperature of the water that goes in the canister and see if that makes a difference.

- What happens when you only put the water in the canister and put it in the tube? Will it fly? What happens if you only put the Alka-Seltzer® in the tube?

Discussion

- What had to happen in order for the film canister to be sent through the air?

- Read Acts 1:8. In our experiment, if the water in the canister represents us, then what does the Alka-Seltzer® represent? (the Holy Spirit) What did the water in the canister need in order for it to go through the air? (the Alka-Seltzer®) God sent the Holy Spirit to fill us, to live in us, so that we would have the power to tell others about His grace and mercy.

- Did all of the canisters go the same distance? This scripture says that some people will go to Jerusalem, which was the city where they were. Some people will go to Judea, which was the area around Jerusalem. Some would go to Samaria, an area outside of Judea, a little further away. And then it says that some would go to the ends of the earth...and that's really far! Do you think you could shoot a canister that far?

- We can't do it on our own and God knew that. He sent the Holy Spirit to give us the power to be His people no matter how far away He sends us.

Stabbed by a Straw
God's Words

Proverbs 4:21 (NLT) - *Don't lose sight of my words. Let them penetrate deep within your heart.*

Lab Equipment

- fresh potato
- drinking straws

Experiment

- Place the potato on a hard flat surface. Hold it firmly with one hand, or place it between two sturdy objects that will prevent it from moving.

- Place the end of the straw up against the potato and try pushing the straw into the potato.

- Now, use your dominant hand to hold onto the straw. Put your thumb across the end of the straw. With a fast, strong downward motion, stab the potato with the straw.

- If the straw does not go into the potato, then try it again with a firmer, stronger motion. The straw should go into the potato at least an inch.

- Try pulling the straw out of the potato.

Observation

- What happened when you tried pushing the straw into the potato the first time?

- What happened when you stabbed the potato?

- How far did the straw go into the potato?

- What surprised you about this experiment? Did you think the straw would bend or crumble?

- Rank the difficulty of removing the straw from the potato, 1-10, one being easy and 10 being difficult.

Discussion

- What does the word penetrate mean? (to go deep inside)

- Is it easy or difficult to take something away when it has penetrated? (difficult)

- What is so much a part of you that it would be difficult for you not to have it as part of your life? Who do you love so much that it would be difficult to even think of not ever loving him or them?

- Read Proverbs 4:21 (NLT).

- What does this verse say we should let penetrate our hearts? (God's words) Where do we find God's words? (in the Bible, through our spiritual teachers and pastors, meditating on God)

- The straw went deep into the potato and it was difficult to remove. God's words should be such a huge part of our lives that they are deep inside our hearts. God wants us to grow to love His words so much that we can't imagine ever being without them!

Standing Upright
Morals

Proverbs 11:11 (NLT) – *Upright citizens bless a city and make it prosper, but the talk of the wicked tears it apart.*

Lab Equipment

- a bottle with a narrow neck (water bottle)
- baking soda
- balloon
- small funnel
- vinegar
- water

Experiment

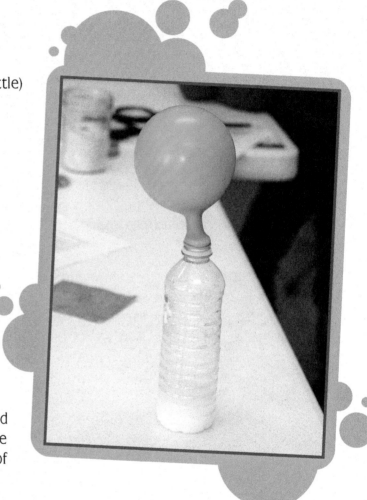

- Push the tip of the funnel into the mouth of the deflated balloon. There should be some space for air to escape. Pour baking soda into the funnel until the balloon is about half full.

- In a small glass, mix the vinegar and water in a 1:1 ratio. Pour this into the bottle until there is about one inch of liquid in the bottom.

- Stretch the opening of the balloon over the mouth of the bottle so that it fits snuggly. As you do this, make sure the baking soda-packed balloon hangs off to the side. You don't want the baking soda to go into the bottle.

- Grasp the neck of the bottle with one hand, holding the balloon in place on the side of the bottle. With the other hand, raise the heavy part of the balloon so that the baking soda dumps into the bottle. Watch what happens!

- The balloon will stand up straight over the bottle and may inflate some.

Observation

- Describe what you heard.

- What did you see happen to the balloon?

- What had to happen in order for the balloon to stand up straight?

Discussion

- When the baking soda was added to the liquid at the bottom of the bottle, the balloon stood upright. Look up the word upright in the dictionary and share the meanings that you found. (It means to be in a vertical position, but it also describes people who live by strict morals.)

- When a person refuses to do anything dishonest, then we say he lives by strict morals because he is honest. What are some other strict morals that make a person upright? (loyalty, faithfulness, fairness, generosity, respectful attitudes)

- What kind of people do you want to live around? What kind of people do you want to govern your city? Read Proverbs 11:11. What kinds of citizens help a city according to this verse? What kind of person hurts a city? Why are upright people good people to have as friends?

- When we live by what God tells us in the Bible, we can't help but live godly, upright lives. The balloon stood upright and you can stand upright also and be glad that your life is modeled after the One who created you.

Stay Dry
Walking with God

Proverbs 4:26 (NLT) – Mark out a straight path for your feet; then stick to the path and stay safe.

Lab Equipment

- aluminum foil
- antiperspirant stick
- glass or metal bowl
- ice
- water

WHEN WE WALK WITH GOD, WE WON'T BE A "DRIP."

Experiment

- Cut a piece of aluminum foil that is big enough to cover the top of the bowl. Across the center, rub the antiperspirant in a line from one edge of the aluminum foil to the other. Keep rubbing until this line is about an inch wide.

- Fill the bowl halfway with ice. Then, add cold water until the water level is about an inch from the upper rim of the bowl.

- Cover the bowl with the piece of aluminum foil, antiperspirant side facing up.

- Watch what happens to the foil.

- Where the antiperspirant is, the foil is dry, but the rest of the foil gets wet.

Observation

- What do you see on the foil?

- What happened to the line of antiperspirant?

Discussion

- In the places where the antiperspirant was rubbed the water beads did not form. It was a line safe from the moisture gathering on the foil.

- Read Proverbs 4:26. What is the path that we should stay on? God has a path for each person's life. When you become a believer you begin walking with God on that path. You leave your sin behind. As long as you walk with God–following what the Bible says and talking with God through prayer–then your path will be free from sin. There will always be sin around you. You'll be tempted to be involved in things that would not please God. People will try to convince you that it's okay to try something just once. Just like the water beads were all around the antiperspirant path, sin will always be within easy reach. But God tells us to stay on the path where we are walking close with Him and we will be safe.

Stem of Life
Evangelism

Matthew 28:19-20 (NLT) - *Therefore, go and make disciples of all the nations, baptizing them in the name of the Father and the Son and the Holy Spirit. Teach these new disciples to obey all the commands I have given you. And be sure of this: I am with you always, even to the end of the age.*

Lab Equipment

- 1 piece of celery
- 1 white carnation
- 2 clear drinking glasses
- blue food coloring
- red food coloring
- water

Experiment

- Pour water into both of the glasses. Use the food coloring to make the water in one glass red and the water in the other glass blue.

- Place the celery in the glass of red water and the white carnation in the glass of blue water.

- Leave these set overnight.

- You should be able to see where the celery was drinking the water, because it has taken on some of the red color. The carnation that was white will now have some blue in the petals.

Observation

- What happened to the celery?

- Slice a piece off the end of the celery that was in the water. Has the entire thing changed color or are there spots of color?

- What happened to the white carnation?

Discussion

- One of the main jobs of plant stems is to carry water from the roots in the soil to the leaves and flowers. You don't usually notice that the water is moving through the stem because water is clear, but when the water has color to it, then you can tell where it is going.

- What would happen if the stem didn't want to do its job? (The plant would die. The flower would wilt.)

- There are people in our neighborhoods that don't know Jesus. Who is going to tell them? There are people in other states who don't know Jesus. Who is going to tell them? There are people on the other side of our world who don't know Jesus. Who is going to tell them? What will happen if no one tells them?

- Read Matthew 28:19-20. This was the very last thing Jesus said before He went back to heaven. If you were going to leave someone you would want your last words to be very important. These words of Jesus are very important. Who was Jesus talking to? These words are also for us. Jesus says that we are the ones who should take the message of God's love and forgiveness to everyone. Just like the stem is the way the water gets from the glass to the flower, we are supposed to be the stem carrying the Living Water that God gives. If the stem doesn't do its job, the plant will die. If we don't do the job God gave us, people will go through life without knowing how different it could be if they made God the center of their lives.

Stick Together
Friend of God

Proverbs 18:24 (NASB) - *A man of many friends comes to ruin, but there is a friend who sticks closer than a brother.*

Lab Equipment

- Borax™
- large spoon
- measuring cups
- tablespoon
- two containers for mixing
- water
- white glue
- Ziploc® bags

Experiment

- Make a solution of Borax™ and water. Add one tablespoon of Borax™ per cup of water. The Borax™ needs to be completely dissolved before it can be used, so after stirring, let it set for 15 minutes.

- Make a solution of half water and half white glue.

- The child should hold the Ziploc® bag open. Pour ¼ cup of the glue mixture into it.

- Add ¼ cup of the Borax™ mixture.

- Immediately, zip the bag closed, trying to get some of the air out as you do.

- Mash and knead the mixture thoroughly.

- Once it turns into a glob of slime, there may be some additional water left in the bag. Carefully, pour this extra water off, and remove the slime from the bag.

- The kids will absolutely love their slime, so take a moment to enjoy their fascination and excitement.

Observation

- Describe the two solutions before they were put in the bag.

- What did the slime look like?

- How did the slime feel?

- Does the slime have a smell?

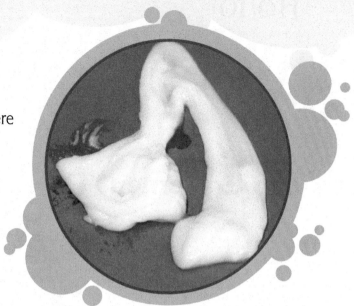

Discussion

- Can you now get the Borax™ and glue solutions apart from one another?

- Read Proverbs 18:24.

- Even the best of friends have their differences and friendships end. Name something that has come between you and your friend. What did you argue about? What does your friend do that hurts your feelings?

- We are close to our friends and we are even closer to our family. But the Bible tells us that God wants to be closer to us than any friend or any member of our family. Will He leave us when we don't understand? Will He leave us when our feelings are hurt? Will He leave us when we are upset or in pain or angry?

- We can't get the Borax™ and white glue apart from one another. They are stuck for good! God wants to be the friend that will never leave us.

- Say, "I am a friend of God!" How does that make you feel?

To extend the life of the slime, store it in the Ziploc® bag in the refrigerator. It will eventually go bad, but now that you know the recipe, you can always make more!

Summer Snow
Honor

Proverbs 26:1 (NLT) - *Honor doesn't go with fools any more than snow with summer or rain with harvest.*

Lab Equipment

- 2 ounces of water
- 5-ounce cup
- Insta-Snow powder (See "Supply Sites" to order this.)
- teaspoon

Experiment

- To make the most impact do this experiment in the summer on a hot day.

- Place a teaspoon of the Insta-Snow powder in the bottom of a 5-ounce cup. Spread it evenly across the bottom.

- Measure out 2 ounces of water in a separate cup.

- Pour the water into the cup with the Insta-Snow powder. Watch closely, because in 5 seconds, you'll see a delightful change.

Observation

- Describe what you saw happen when the water was added to the cup.

- Touch the snow. Describe how it feels. Is it cold? What surprised you about the way it felt?

Discussion

- Insta-Snow is what the artificial ski slopes are now using so that skiers can ski even when the weather hasn't cooperated.

- Name some things that go with winter. Now, name some things that go with summer.

- What time of year are you supposed to get snow? Why is it strange to be making snow at this time of year? (Snow isn't supposed to happen in the summertime!)

- Look up Proverbs 26:1.

- What does it mean to be foolish? What kinds of things does a foolish person do?

- What does it mean to be honorable? (When someone is honorable, the people around them show them respect. People look up to them and admire them.)

- Can someone be foolish and honorable at the same time? That sounds ridiculous! We don't respect people who are foolish and make bad decisions; we respect people who make good choices and who are honorable. The two traits–being foolish and being honorable–don't go together, just like snow and summer don't go together.

Sweet Understanding
Word of God

Psalm 119:103-104 (NLT) - *How sweet are your words to my taste; they are sweeter than honey. Your commandments give me understanding; no wonder I hate every false way of life.*

Lab Equipment

- 2 cups water
- 4 cups sugar
- cotton string
- galvanized washer
- glass jar
- honey
- large spoon
- pencil
- saucepan
- waxed paper

Experiment

- Mix the water and sugar together in the saucepan. Heat over a medium-high heat until it comes to a boil. Keep stirring the entire time. The sugar will dissolve in the water and become clear. Bring it to a rolling boil.

- Carefully pour the solution into the jar and cover the jar with some waxed paper.

- Tie the washer to one end of a piece of string and the pencil to the other end. Depending on how tall your jar is the string will vary in length–it should be about two-thirds the height of the jar when the washer and pencil are attached.

- Dip the string in the sugary solution. Lay the string out straight on a piece of waxed paper. Leave it there to dry for 2 days.

- On the third day, remove the waxed paper covering on the jar. Gently drop the washer into the solution and place the pencil across the mouth of the jar. Leave the jar still for seven days! Avoid the temptation to touch any part of the experiment. This works only if the jar is undisturbed.

- At the end of the seven days, there should be sugar crystals forming on the string. Pull it out of the solution and let it dry on a piece of waxed paper. Now, for the test...taste what has accumulated on the string. Then, taste a little honey.

- For a variation, try adding some food coloring or special flavoring to the rolling boil.

Observation

- How did you know that the sugar was completely dissolved in the water?

- Describe the string on the first day. Describe what the water looked like when it first started heating and then when it was poured in the jar.

- What did you see after the string had been suspended in the solution for three days?

- What did the string look like after hanging in the solution for seven days?

- What did it taste like? Have you ever had anything that tastes similar to this? Was it soft or brittle when you bit into it? How hard was it to bite through?

- How did the honey and the rock candy compare?

Discussion

- What we have made is old-fashioned rock candy. It is one of the oldest kinds of candy and was first used as a medicine. Now that's a great kind of medicine!

- The rock candy is very sweet. Read Psalm 119:103-104. What does this verse call sweet? What is sweet about God's words?

- What has the Word of God, the Bible, helped you understand? How do you feel when you understand something that you didn't understand before? It's a sweet feeling!

The Glowing Pickle
God's Power

1 Peter 5:11 (NLT) - *All power is his forever and ever. Amen.*

Lab Equipment

- 2, 16-penny nails
- a wood plank
- electrician's tape
- large dill pickle
- sharp knife
- short extension cord

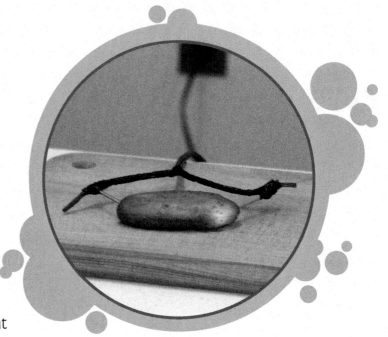

Experiment

- Do not tell the children that you are going to be making a pickle light up. The initial part of their discussion will be about what they thought was going to happen.

- Cut off the end of the extension cord that does not have the plug on it. Slice through the plastic covering and separate the two wires about 6". Peel back the plastic coating to expose about 1" of both wires.

- Wrap each exposed wire around the head of a 16-penny nail. Then, completely cover the exposed wires with electrician's tape.

- Insert a nail into each end of the pickle. The nails should not touch one another inside the pickle. From this point on, do not touch the metal of the nail! You could experience more of this experiment than you want to.

- Lay the pickle on a wood plank (or any nonmetal surface).

- Plug the extension cord into a socket and turn out the lights.

- Wait for a few seconds and you'll notice that the pickle is glowing!

Observation

• Which senses did you use to experience this experiment? Did you smell anything? Did you hear anything? Did you see anything? We do not want you to use the sense of touch while the pickle is plugged in. (Did that sound as strange to you as it did to me?)

Discussion

• Was any part of the experiment a little scary to you? What did you think was going to happen when the cord was plugged in?

• Where was the power to light up the pickle coming from? Could you see the power? What did you think of this experiment?

• Do you know what the Bible says about God's power? Read 1 Peter 5:11. It says that ALL power is God's; it always has been and it always will be. Tell something else you know about God's power.

• Think of some of the Bible stories you know that are amazing because of God's power. Tell how the people saw God's power at work in each one. (Jesus' resurrection and ascension, the Israelites crossing the Red Sea, Daniel in the lions' den, Gideon going into battle, the Israelites taking Jericho, Paul and Silas in jail, Lazarus raised from the dead... and you can take it from here!) Do you think some of those people were a little scared? Do you think they expected God to work in the way that He did?

• We couldn't see the power that lit up the pickle, but we saw what happened. We can't see God's power, but we can see what it does. We see the change in lives when people give themselves to the Lord and we see what happens when people pray. How would you describe God's power?

Through the Clouds
Sadness & Disappointment

Psalm 36:5 (NLT) - *Your unfailing love, O Lord, is as vast as the heavens; your faithfulness reaches beyond the clouds.*

Lab Equipment

- an overcast day
- energy beads

Experiment

Kids absolutely love energy beads and are amazed at how quickly they see a reaction in them. Don't pass up this fun opportunity...order some today! (See the resource page at the back of the book for information on where they can be purchased.) They look like a bag of white pony beads you would buy at a craft store, but don't be fooled. You will also need an overcast, gloomy day to do this activity.

- Give each child five beads while you are indoors. Tell the children to make a fist around the beads and not open their hand until you give them the signal.

- Now, go outside. The children will describe what kind of day it is. (Their hands are still closed.) Would you say this is a sunny day? I don't even think the sun is shining, and that's a problem for our experiment because the beads react to the rays from the sun.

- Let's try it anyway. The children will open their hands out flat with the beads resting in their palm. Watch the beads closely as soon as you open your hand.

- The beads will turn colors in a matter of 5 seconds!

Observation

- What happened to the beads?

- What were you expecting them to do?

- Are all the beads the same color?

- Compare your beads to the ones your neighbor has.

- Can you see the sun?

- Close your hand for a minute and see what happens to your beads.

DON'T HAVE ENERGY BEADS? TURN TO PAGE 124.

Discussion

- If the beads change color because of the sun's ultraviolet (UV) rays, then what must be happening? (We can't see the ultraviolet rays from the sun, but they are coming through and are very powerful.)

- Read Psalm 36:5. What does that verse mean to you?

- How would you compare this experiment to the way God works in our lives? If the sun represents God and we are the beads, what would the gloomy clouds be?

- Name a time when you were really disappointed. How did you feel about God at that time? Did you feel excited about what God was doing? Did you feel a little gloomy? But, was God there with you in spite of the disappointment? It may have been later on–the next day or a week after–when you realized that God had been working in the situation to make something good out of it. The ultraviolet rays from the sun made their way through the grey clouds to change the beads into bright colors. God reaches through our gloominess, our sadness, our grief, to change us into His beautiful people.

- When we hid the beads from the sun what happened to them? How is that like when we shut ourselves off from God?

Throw to Grow
Holy Living

Hebrews 12:1 (NIV) - *Therefore, since we are surrounded by such a great cloud of witnesses, let us throw off everything that hinders and the sin that so easily entangles, and let us run with perseverance the race marked out for us.*

Lab Equipment

- cereal (such as Cheerios®)
- craft stick (or tongue depressor)
- pencil
- several different colored markers
- yard stick or measuring tape

Experiment

- Place a pencil on a table and then lay the craft stick across the pencil. With one of the markers, make a mark on the craft stick to indicate where the pencil is underneath. This is called the fulcrum.

- Place a piece of cereal on the end of the craft stick that is resting against the table. Hit the other end of the craft stick with your fist and see how far the piece of cereal goes.

- Measure the distance from the fulcrum to where the cereal landed. Write down that distance with the same color marker as the mark you put on the craft stick.

- Now, change where the craft stick rests against the pencil; change the fulcrum. Mark it with a different color of marker. Place a piece of cereal on the end of the craft stick and hit it again. Measure the distance and record it with the color of marker used to mark the fulcrum.

- Repeat this process marking different fulcrums—the point where the craft stick rests on the pencil.

Observation

- How did the position of the fulcrum affect the distance that the cereal went?

- Which fulcrum sent the cereal the furthest? Which one sent it the shortest?

- What do you think would happen if you used a ruler instead of a craft stick? Or something larger than a pencil?

Discussion

- Read Hebrews 12:1. Which phrase in this verse reminds you of our experiment?

- Name some things that we are to "throw off." (ideas, opinions, habits, actions that are not pleasing to God)

- What are we supposed to do with those things we just listed?

- Which one of the fulcrums would you want to use to throw off the things we named? We want them to go far away and out of our lives.

- This scripture tells us why we want to throw away those things. What does it say is the reason? (Those things will tangle us up if we keep them. We want to be able to run the race that God has for us, living the full life He has for us.)

* For some added fun, try to make the cereal land in a large cup or deli container.

Tight Squeeze
Peer Pressure

Romans 12:2 (J.B. Phillips) - *Don't let the world around you squeeze you into its own mould, but let God re-mould your minds from within.*

Lab Equipment

- boiled egg
- glass bottle (cappuccino bottle is great)
- matches
- newspaper

Experiment

- You need a glass bottle with a mouth noticeably smaller than the egg. A cappuccino bottle works wonderfully. Wash it and allow the inside to completely dry.

- Gently remove the shell from the boiled egg. Place egg on the mouth of the bottle and show that it will not go into the bottle.

- Twist a piece of newspaper to make a small 6" long torch.

- Light the end of the newspaper. Make sure it is going to stay lit and then place it down in the bottle. As soon as you are sure the paper is going to continue to burn, set the egg on the mouth of the bottle. Step back and watch what happens.

- When the paper is burned completely and goes out the egg will be sucked into the bottle.

Observation

- What happened when the egg was set on the bottle the first time?

- What happened to the egg the second time when the flame went out on the newspaper torch?

- Will the egg come back out of the bottle now?

Discussion

- How did the egg get through the opening of the bottle? (It was squeezed.)

- Is it easy or difficult to get the egg back out of the bottle? (difficult, you have to ruin the egg to get it out)

- Read Romans 12:2 from the J.B. Phillips Translation. (It is very important to read from this translation because of the words that are used.) What does this verse warn us against?

- How does the world squeeze you into its mold? What would the world like you to think about movies? What would the world like you to think about using curse words? What would the world like you to think about money? (The world tries to talk us into living ways that displease God. Our minds are squeezed into accepting those ideas and believing they are okay.)

- Have you ever had friends who tried to get you to do something that you knew was wrong? What did they try to get you to do? How did that make you feel? Did you feel like they might not be your friends if you said no?

- Just like it's difficult to get the egg back out of the bottle, it's difficult to stop believing the way the world has taught us once we let our minds be molded by it.

- What can you do to keep the world from squeezing you into its mold?

Unscrew the Ears of Your Heart

Listening to God

Matthew 13:12 (NLT) - *To those who are open to my teaching, more understanding will be given, and they will have an abundance of knowledge. But to those who are not listening, even what they have will be taken away from them.*

Lab Equipment

- empty can with a screw-on or snap-on lid
- hammer
- large pitcher of water
- large tub
- nail

Experiment

- On one side toward the bottom of the can, punch a hole using the nail and hammer.

- Hold the can over the tub. One of the children should place a finger over the hole while you fill the can with water. When the can is full screw on the cap. The child can now remove her finger.

- Remove the cap. Put the cap back on. Remove the cap. Put the cap back on.

- When the cap is on, the water will not flow. When the cap is off, the water comes out the hole.

Observation

- What happened when the child removed her finger from the hole?

- What happened when the cap was removed?

- What happened when the cap was screwed on again?

Discussion

- Read Matthew 13:12. What connections can you make between this verse and the experiment?

- When was the can like someone who is listening to God? (When the cap was unscrewed and the water was flowing.)

- When was the can like someone who had closed his or her heart to God? (When the cap was screwed on and the water was not flowing.)

- What does this verse say is given to those people who listen to God? (understanding, knowledge)

- God wants to talk with us. He wants to help us live our lives with His direction in mind. Living God's plan is better than living our own plan. But if we don't listen to God, then we won't know what steps He wants us to take. Sometimes we think we know what God wants, even without praying about it. Why do people jump ahead of God sometimes? (They get in a hurry. They start thinking they know what's best.) More than anything, God wants to keep moving in your life, but He can only do that if you listen to Him. Listening to God is like unscrewing the cap so the water can flow. When we pay attention to what God is saying, He teaches us.

Unusual Light
Light of the World

John 12:46 (NLT) - *I have come as a light to shine in this dark world, so that all who put their trust in me will no longer remain in the darkness.*

Lab Equipment

- cooler
- dry ice
- heavy black plastic (possibly)
- light stick (any color)
- pitcher of water

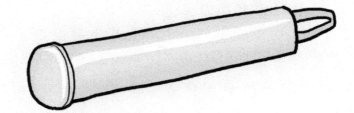

Experiment

- Make sure the room can be completely darkened. Places that are letting in light can be covered with heavy black plastic you get at a home improvement store. Light sticks can usually be found in the novelty and party section of a discount department store. The best time to get them is in the fall because kids use them when they trick or treat. Be extremely careful handling dry ice. Wear heavy gloves and do not let the children close enough to touch it. You can create awesome effects using dry ice, but it is so cold it will burn your skin. Many grocery stores carry dry ice, but you'll want to take your gloves and a cooler to the store when you go to purchase it.

- Because the room is pitch dark, you must know where everything is before the lights are turned out. Place the dry ice in a cooler that has a lift-off lid, but keep the lid on until the lights go out. You may want to have your hand on the pitcher with the light stick sitting beside it.

- Turn out the lights. Lift the lid off the cooler. Slowly pour some of the water onto the dry ice. Snap the light stick and drop it into the cooler. Gently blow into the cooler.

- An eerie mist will rise from the cooler that lights up, according to the color of your light stick.

Observation

- What happened when the water was poured into the cooler?

- What changed when the light stick was put in the cooler?

- How did the room change once the water was poured on the dry ice and the light stick was added?

Discussion

- How did you feel when the room was completely dark? How did you feel once the light came from the cooler? What would happen if you tried to walk around in the darkness?

- The Bible tells us that everyone has sinned—everyone has disobeyed God; everyone has displeased Him. Sin makes our world dark. The Bible also calls Jesus the Light of the World. Read John 12:46. The dark room in our experiment represents the sin that is all around us in this world. What part of the experiment do you relate to Jesus? What does this verse tell us we have to do in order not to be in the darkness of sin any longer?

- It would be terribly difficult to live in a place that was dark all the time. You would probably get lost a lot. You'd have bruises and cuts from running into things. You would feel lonely not being able to see other people. When light comes into the room everything changes! Living without Jesus is lonely. You feel lost because you're not doing what God created you to do. When you put your trust in Jesus, then everything changes. You go from living in darkness to living with the Light of the World.

What's on Your Label?
Fruit of the Spirit

Galatians 5:22-23 - *But the fruit of the Spirit is love, joy, peace, patience, kindness, goodness, faithfulness, gentleness and self-control. Against such things there is no law.*

Lab Equipment

- Ingredient labels from foods

Experiment (Game)

- Take the label off of at least eight foods and cut around the ingredient lists. Leave any hint of identification off (logo, brand, food). Number each label and then write on a separate piece of paper the same number along with the name of the food. This is your cheat-sheet. Suggested foods are: ketchup, cake mix, macaroni and cheese, cottage cheese, ravioli, cereal, graham crackers, whipped topping, noodles, mayonnaise.

- Give the children a piece of paper with the same numbers listed down the left side and the names of the foods across the top (without their numbers). The kids will look at the ingredients and try to determine which food belongs to which label and then write that food name next to the appropriate number on their sheet.

Observation

Packaged foods often contain additives and chemicals that prevent the foods from spoiling or they enhance the flavor.

- Were you able to identify the food being described by just the ingredients?

- Were there any surprises? Which ones?

- Were there more ingredients or fewer ingredients than you expected?

Discussion

- What would happen if we removed one ingredient? (The food wouldn't be the same. Every ingredient helps make the food what it is supposed to be.)

- Write down the ingredients that make up a believer in Jesus.

- Look up Galatians 5:22-23. God sends the Holy Spirit to give us gifts that we are known by. These gifts identify us as believers. What does this verse say should be on our ingredient label? (Love, joy, peace, patience, kindness, goodness, faithfulness, gentleness, and self-control.)

- What would happen if we removed one of those gifts from our lives? (We wouldn't be all that God wants us to be.)

marshmallow, graham crackers, tomato sauce, vegetable soup, cereal, cream cheese icing, chow mein noodles, whipped topping

1.
2.
3.
4.
5.
6.
7.
8.

Supply Sites
Where to Find the Hard-to-Find Items

Most of the items needed for the experiments in this book can be found around your home or at the local discount department store. A few of the items, however, are not so readily available. The following list will help you acquire supplies you may not be familiar with or that you don't know where to find. If ordering online, allow 10-14 days for delivery.

Airzooka

www.zerotoys.com

Blacklight – purchase at your local discount department store's lighting department

Borax – purchase at your local grocery store with the laundry detergents

Cellophane (yellow)

www.papermart.com

1.800.745.8800

Dry Ice – purchase at large grocery stores

Energy Beads

www.stevespanglerscience.com

1.800.223.9080

Eyedroppers

www.dharmatrading.com

1.800.542.5227

Flash Paper

www.starlight.com/pyrotechnics

1.800.275.4800

Glow Powder

www.stevespanglerscience.com

1.800.223.9080

Insta-Snow

www.stevespanglerscience.com

1.800.223.9080

Magnet Wand

www.discountschoolsupply.com

1.800.627.2829

Nature Print Paper

www.ssww.com

1.800.243.9232

Slush Powder (Lightning Gel)

www.williamsmagic.com

1.520.790.4060

Test Tubes

Purchase at your local teacher supply store or www.stevespanglerscience.com

Index
Scripture References

Index
(Continued)

CPSIA information can be obtained
at www.ICGtesting.com
Printed in the USA
LVOW06s1136160816

500583LV00004B/5/P